AR STUDIES IN HISTORY

Editor: Patrick Richardson

British Foreign Policy in the Age of Palmerston

M.E. Chamberlain

LONGMAN

LONGMAN GROUP LIMITED
Longman House,
Burnt Mill, Harlow, Essex CM20 2JE, England
and Associated Companies throughout the World.

First published 1980
Third impression 1984

ISBN 0 582 35257 6

Set in 10/11 Press Roman, IBM

Printed in Hong Kong by
Wilture Printing Co., Ltd.

We are grateful to the following for permission to reproduce copyright material:

Cambridge University Press for extracts from *The Foundation of British Foreign Policy* by H. Temperley and L.M. Penson (1958).

The cartoon on the cover is reproduced by permission of Punch Publications.

Contents

Introduction to the series

The seminar method of teaching is being used increasingly. It is a way of learning in smaller groups through discussion, designed both to get away from and to supplement the basic lecture techniques. To be successful, the members of a seminar must be informed – or else, in the unkind phrase of a cynic – it can be a 'pooling of ignorance'. The chapter in the textbook of English or European history by its nature cannot provide material in this depth, but at the same time the full academic work may be too long and perhaps too advanced.

For this reason we have invited practising teachers to contribute short studies on specialised aspects of British and European history with these special needs in mind. For this series the authors have been asked to provide, in addition to their basic analysis, a full selection of documentary material of all kinds and an up-to-date and comprehensive bibliography. Both these sections are referred to in the text, but it is hoped that they will prove to be valuable teaching and learning aids in themselves.

Note on the System of References:
A bold number in round brackets (5) in the text refers the reader to the corresponding entry in the Bibliography section at the end of the book. A bold number in square brackets, preceded by 'doc' [docs. 6,8] refers the reader to the corresponding items in the section of Documents, which follows the main text.

PATRICK RICHARDSON
General Editor

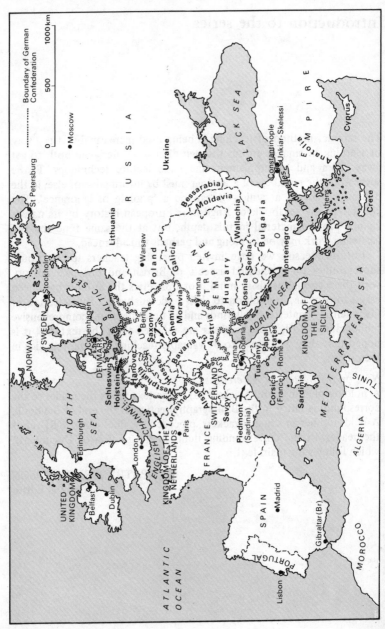

Europe in 1815

Part One: The Background

1 The Concepts of Foreign Policy

Britain is a western European country. She shares with the other powers of western Europe a common heritage, derived ultimately from the civilisations of Greece, Rome and Judaea. She had been part of western Christendom and had participated in the long and complex evolution of the idea of a *ius gentium* or Law of Nations. She shared the experience of the Renaissance, the scientific revolution and the age of reason, all of which brought about changes in thinking about the right relationship of man to man and of nation to nation. British statesmen in the nineteenth century rarely tried to make these principles explicit – William Gladstone in the latter half of the century came closest to doing so – but they had a common body of assumptions about the right conduct of international affairs which they shared with most continental statesmen (69). They were often puzzled and sometimes resentful when they came into contact with men of other civilisations, such as the Chinese, who did not share the same heritage [doc. 53].

At the same time there were distinctive features in the British experience. Her geographical position on the edge of north-western Europe meant that, since the age of discovery, her thoughts and interests had turned outwards towards the Americas, the Indian Ocean and the Pacific. This did not mean that Britain could afford to disregard what was happening in continental Europe. It has been amply demonstrated that 'splendid isolation' was never a preferred, or even for long a practicable, British policy (50). But it did mean that by the early nineteenth century no other European great power was so committed to worldwide interests as was Britain.

This was connected with another way in which British experience differed from the continental. By 1815 Britain was already well advanced along the path of the first industrial revolution, a revolution which had been accompanied by a great increase in population and the herding of a large part of that population into the new industrial towns, with a host of social problems which, because they were quite unprecedented in the experience of any country, were totally baffling to a British government accustomed to the constitutional equilibrium which had been achieved in eighteenth-century Britain. Industrialisation meant dangers as well as opportunities. Britain could no longer feed her own people. She was dependent on international trade both for food and for the raw materials necessary to keep her industry going: any interference with trade was an immediate and serious threat [doc. 55]. To protect her trade routes Britain felt that she must be supreme at sea. She always insisted that British command of the seas must by its nature be defensive since she had no large army with which to invade other powers but this argument was by no means universally accepted by other powers (102, 8). Britain also felt compelled to insist on a very strong definition of her maritime rights, even when some modification might have led to other benefits [docs. 12, 38].

The industrial revolution had led to a changed social structure in Britain. A large and powerful middle class had emerged which was both educated and articulate. The processes by which power was transferred to it from the traditionally dominant landed classes were leisurely, and indeed incomplete, in the nineteenth century, but it produced its own leaders in men like Richard Cobden and John Bright [docs. 5, 51, 53]. Lord Castlereagh admitted as early as 1820 that in Britain, unlike say Russia, there was a public opinion which could not be flouted for long by any government [doc. 19]. His successors, George Canning and Lord Palmerston, made conscious efforts to win and direct that public opinion by the publication of documents explaining their policy and by communications to the press (94). Public opinion was not always well informed; it could become wildly excited, as at the time of the Crimean War (62), but its prejudices were by no means ignoble. It was firmly convinced of the superiority of British to continental institutions and this enabled both Canning and Palmerston, when they chose to do so, to appeal for public sympathy for 'constitutional' states [docs. 20, 25–27, 44, 54b]. It also had a humanitarian prejudice in favour of the abolition of the Slave Trade and ultimately of slavery itself. Castlereagh felt compelled to press the first at the Congress of Vienna and Palmerston derived great public support for his campaign against it [doc. 34].

Constitutionally, Britain did differ from the other great powers of Europe. Many European countries had developed some form of representative institutions in the Middle Ages but most of these had succumbed to the establishment of absolute monarchies in the period after the Renaissance. Britain, alone of the great powers, not only saved but developed her parliamentary institutions in the seventeenth century. British statesmen who were regarded as arch-conservatives at home, such as Lord Castlereagh, looked back with satisfaction to 1688, and could scarcely condemn all revolutions out of hand when their own constitution was founded on one. The greater flexibility of the British system enabled them to escape revolution at home between 1789 and 1815. Fears generated by the French Revolution held back the cause of reform but as calmer times returned British politicians came to believe that reform would stave off revolution. Holding such views they could not share continental leaders' fears that all political change was dangerous (57). Nevertheless they distinguished carefully between movements for constitutional reform, which they generally considered good, and movements for attacks on property, which they saw as subversive of all social order. 'Democracy' was a term of abuse, not of approbation, in the mouths of early nineteenth-century statesmen [doc. 19] only those who had a 'stake in the country', usually proved by the possession of substantial property, were, it was considered, to be trusted with a say in the government.

Nostalgia sometimes sees Britain as the greatest power in the world in the nineteenth century. She was never that. It is true that her overseas interests had compelled her to assume the role of a world as well as of a European power but in terms of the continent of Europe she was always only one among five great powers, Britain, France, Austria, Russia and Prussia. A.J.P. Taylor has suggested that the test of a great power, that which distinguishes it from a minor power, is its strength for war, its ability to make a respectable showing in a contest of the great powers (88). The five great powers of early nineteenth-century Europe had very different strengths and weaknesses. British power was known to be naval and commercial. Russian power lay mainly in her huge reserves of manpower; the crucial question was whether she would ever be able to organise and bring these resources to bear. Prussia, on the contrary, made up in organisation what she initially lacked in population. Austria had a large population and large resources but the hetereogenous nature of her empire made its strength suspect. France, even after the defeats of 1814–15, still seemed to be potentially the strongest continental power, with the advantages of national unity and a strong military tradition. Even a great power could not really 'go it alone', its security and influence depended to a significant extent on its relations with the other great powers, on where it would find itself in the groupings of Europe (40).

The idea of a Concert of Europe became an important concept in the course of the nineteenth century. According to Dr Holbraad the word 'concert' was first used in the 1790s but it then had only the general meaning of a 'temporary political situation implying some agreement between the parties'. In the early nineteenth century it was used interchangeably with a number of other terms, such as 'the European system', 'the confederacy', or 'the great alliance', or 'the union' **(48)**. Initially these meant quite specifically the coalition against Napoleonic France but gradually they came to acquire the meaning of a permanent relationship between the great powers of Europe **(3)**.

It is important to distinguish between the idea of a semi-institutionalised relationship between all the great powers of Europe which might come into play to settle all disputes and problems, and the much more limited idea of a coalition between certain powers to safeguard certain specific interests. Both ideas are to be found in the diplomacy of nineteenth-century Europe. The English philosopher Thomas Hobbes (1558–1679) had described a 'state of nature' before society was organised, when each individual lived in conflict with his neighbour, acknowledging no superior authority or law. Most historians and anthropologists would doubt whether men as individuals ever lived in such a state but it has been suggested that this would describe quite accurately the relationship between sovereign states. By definition a sovereign body has no superior, and international 'law' could be regarded as merely a set of convenient conventions which, in the case of dissent, could not be enforced by any outside authority. This is not a bad description of the actual state of international relations in nineteenth-century Europe, but there were alternative traditions dating back to the Middle Ages when the idea of western Christendom (itself deriving from the unity of the Roman empire) had not yet been fragmented by the rise of strong national states. Tsar Alexander I of Russia had a mystic idea of the continuing unity of Christendom and the way in which this could be translated into a system of international law and organisation [**doc. 4**]. His mysticism aroused the impatience of more practical men like Lord Castlereagh or the Austrian Chancellor, Metternich, and the obvious danger of perverting such a vision in favour of a particular political stance (in Alexander's case firm attachment to the *status quo* and Russian interests) created deep distrust among patriots and liberals of other countries. Nevertheless, Alexander and the great British Prime Minister, William Pitt, discussed the future organisation of Europe in 1805 and this exchange of ideas contained the germ of many future developments [**doc. 1**].

The philosophical idea took on more reality as the century advanced. The term 'the Concert of Europe' (*le concert européen*) first appeared in a treaty in the Treaty of Paris of 1856 at the end of the Crimean War **(3)**, [**doc. 52**]. William Gladstone spoke of it frequently in the 1870s as a reality of European political organisation – a change implicitly acknowledged by *Hansard* which had previously used the form 'concert' with a small 'c', but now began to use it as a proper name, 'Concert' **(48)**. It was a profoundly important idea which led eventually to the League of Nations and its successor, the United Nations as well as to the European Economic Community, because basically it embodied the concept that nations do not necessarily live in a 'state of nature' one towards the other but can cooperate on agreed terms, create international institutions properly so-called, and even eventually surrender some of their sovereignty to those institutions.

However important the idea was ultimately to prove, its development and acceptance in the nineteenth century was extremely slow. The 'Concert' frequently reverted to being a coalition for specific purposes. When the government of most European countries was in the hands of conservative monarchs the Concert tended to be a device for maintaining the *status quo*, and then found itself in conflict with another, and in the nineteenth century more powerful, trend in European history – the growth of the idea of nationality [**docs. 5, 8**].

William Pitt had hoped that on the restoration of peace they would be able to re-establish 'a general System of Public Law in Europe' and come to a general agreement 'for the mutual protection and Security of different Powers' [**doc. 1**]. A tentative beginning was made in setting up such a system in the Treaty of Chaumont of 1 March 1814 and the Treaty of Quadruple Alliance of 20 November 1815 [**docs. 2, 3**]. But it soon became clear that Britain's interpretation of the purpose of the alliance differed from that of the three eastern powers, Austria, Prussia and Russia, and after 1820 from that of France too. Britain believed that the alliance could only properly be invoked to defend the particular settlement arrived at in 1814–15 by the treaties of Vienna and Paris at the end of the Napoleonic wars. It was never intended 'as an Union for the Government of the World or for the Superintendence of the Internal Affairs of other States' [**doc. 19**].

The three eastern powers had a much wider concept of the use to which they could put the alliance. They wished to use it for nothing less than the defence of the whole existing structure of society **(57)**. The French Revolution had badly frightened all the property-owning classes of Europe, and whereas in the eighteenth century the aristocracy had flirted with ideas of republicanism and anti-clericalism, looking on them as interesting new philosophies, now they turned against them, believing their inevitable outcome to be blood-stained anarchy. Conservatism and respect for 'legitimate' authority revived as a political creed and found its prophets and theorists [**doc. 9**]. Moreover revolutionary tendencies were considered to be infectious. The eastern powers claimed the right to intervene in other states to nip such dangers in the bud [doc. 18].

Britain and the other powers could agree when it came to the containment of France. France was doubly dangerous. First, it was there that monarchy had been overthrown and the new ideals of republicanism, egalitarianism, democracy and anti-clericalism had temporarily triumphed; these new ideals had been carried to many parts of Europe by the revolutionary and Napoleonic armies. Secondly, the Revolution had been succeeded by the military despotism of Napoleon, who had far surpassed Louis XIV in his ambitions and aggressions against other European powers. France then was not only the home of disturbing new philosophies, she was also an ambitious and powerful military state. Wariness of France remained a constant factor in British foreign policy in the nineteenth century, even when the two powers were outwardly on cordial terms [docs. 36, 39].

Britain was therefore happy to agree with the other powers on those terms of the Vienna Settlement (discussed in more detail in Chapter 2) which provided France with strong neighbours. Generally speaking she had no objection to the restoration, where possible, of legitimate rulers and governments who had been displaced by the revolutionary and Napoleonic wars. The principle of legitimacy did not have such a strong ideological appeal to the British government as to the eastern powers but in fact all the powers were prepared to depart from it when it conflicted with other national interests or ambitions [docs. 11, 14]. The statesmen at Vienna were above all seeking peace and security. Europe had just endured nearly a quarter of a century of almost continuous warfare. Stability seemed to be the most desirable good of all.

British statesmen believed that the Vienna Settlement had created a desirable balance in Europe (40). Some men, like Richard Cobden, believed that the 'balance of power' had become a shibboleth of British foreign policy [doc. 5]. In fact, British Foreign Secretaries, particularly Lord Palmerston, did use the phrase constantly [docs. 6, 26, 45]. It is important, however, to note that the phrase has changed its meaning in the twentieth century. Today it normally means a balance between two power blocs, for example the balance between Russia and America and their respective allies during the Cold War, and this was also its meaning just before the First World War. The then British Foreign Secretary, Sir Edward Grey, provided the classic definition of this form of balance when he wrote, 'I imagine it to mean that when one Power or group of Powers is the strongest "bloc" in Europe, our [the British] policy has been, or should be, that of creating, or siding with, some other combination of Powers, in order to make a counterpoise to the strongest Power or Group and so to preserve equilibrium in Europe.' Its meaning in the period after 1815 was somewhat different. The allies then meant the territorial balance created between the great powers by the settlement. So long as no power seriously diverged from this, it was believed that peace could be preserved. There were no permanent blocs. France sided with Britain on the Iberian Peninsula in 1834 [doc. 26] but she had sided with the eastern powers on Spain in 1822. Britain sided with Russia against France over the Eastern Question in 1840 [doc. 30] but with France against Russia in 1854; Austria, despite her dependence on Russian help to subdue revolution in 1849, began to side with Britain and France against Russia in 1855. All combinations were possible and everything depended on the particular issue. This made for a potentially open and flexible system which statesmen hoped would be self-balancing. The fact that there was no major European war for more than a generation after 1815 has made many historians believe that they came close to realising their aim in this respect [doc. 17].

There were, however, those in the nineteenth century, as in the twentieth, who unreservedly condemned both the balance of power and the Vienna Settlement itself [doc. 16]. The Settlement had been made and maintained, they contended, purely for the interests of dynasties and the privileged classes with no concern for national feelings or the new forces rising in society. It is difficult to consider this question except through the distorting glass of hindsight [doc. 20]. The nineteenth century was to prove a revolutionary one in both economic and social terms. Most countries in western Europe underwent industrial revolutions sooner or later; populations doubled and doubled again; ideas changed profoundly on questions such as the franchise. Principles such as national identity and self-determination, which had been ignored at Vienna came to be regarded as almost sacred, yet until late in the century conservatives could argue with truth that national feelings affected only an intellectual minority in, say, Italy.

Britain was satisfied by the Treaty of Vienna. She had no territorial or other ambitions to pursue on the continent of Europe, and so long as general peace was maintained, British trade could be carried on unhindered. On the other hand, she was prepared to see the Vienna Settlement altered if its basic aims were still fulfilled. Thus, she was ready to see Belgium become independent in the 1830s [docs. 25] if its neutrality was guaranteed. Palmerston would have been glad to see Austria withdraw from Italy provided French influence was still effectively excluded [docs. 44, 54]. By 1848 Palmerston plainly regarded some parts of the 1814-15 Settlement as obsolete. He was prepared to accept the establishment first of a Republic and subsequently of a Bonaparte in power in France without any thought of activating an automatic alliance against her (78), [doc. 43]. But even as late as 1863 he refused Napoleon III's invitation to a congress on Poland on the grounds that it seemed designed to lead to a general revision of the Treaty of Vienna which he, Palmerston, still regarded as 'the basis of the existing arrangements of Europe' [doc. 58]. France had been to some extent a 'revisionist' power ever since the First Treaty of Paris of 30 May 1814 had deprived her of her 'natural frontiers' of the Rhine, the Alps and the Pyrenees, secured during the revolutionary wars. Russia had become a revisionist power after the Treaty of Paris of 1856 had imposed humiliating conditions on her freedom of action in the Black Sea [doc. 52]: she was only able to secure their abrogation during the Franco-Prussian war of 1870–71. In contrast, Britain never took the initiative in changing European settlements.

The British approach to foreign policy was always empirical. Frederick the Great once complained, 'the British have no system' (69). A later British Foreign Secretary, Lord Salisbury, suggested that 'English policy is to float lazily downstream, occasionally putting out a diplomatic boat-hook to avoid collisions'. There were, however, certain underlying principles of British foreign policy which Professor Platt suggests can be summed up as 'Security and Trade' (72). This is not to say that Foreign Secretaries, or high Foreign Office officials, had any particular expertise on trading questions, nor that they believed that it was the government's job to seek any special favours for British traders, but they did accept that the British government had a responsibility to see that British trade could be carried on in as many parts of the world as possible without let or hindrance. This was the time when free trade doctrines came to assume almost the force of a gospel in Britain. To men like Richard Cobden and John Bright, free trade was not simply a convenient economic doctrine but the way to international peace, when destructive competition, which was all too likely to lead to war, would be replaced by trade, to mutual advantage. The Manchester School, as Cobden, Bright and their followers came to be called, rose to be an important group of thinkers on foreign policy, as well as on economic questions (89), [docs. 5, 51].

The foundations of British foreign policy in the nineteenth century were laid during the traumatic upheavals of the French revolutionary and Napoleonic wars. Three men provided the guidelines, William Pitt the Younger, George (later Viscount) Canning and Robert Stewart, Viscount Castlereagh.

William Pitt first became Prime Minister in 1783 and retained that office, except for the years 1801–04, until his death in 1806. He came to power by the wish of the king, George III, in the face of the opposition of a hostile House of Commons, but he made good his position by winning the election of 1784. His great asset was his family name. His father, the elder Pitt, first Earl of Chatham, was associated in the public mind with the great victories of the Seven Years War which had left England triumphant over France in both India and North America, although when his son came to power some of those victories had been nullified by the American War of Independence, which had ended in the British recognition of the United States by the Treaty of Versailles of 1783. The first ten years of Pitt's premiership were concerned with domestic, Indian and colonial issues rather than with European ones, although his successful intervention to diminish French influence in the United Provinces in 1787 and his unsuccessful attempts to induce the Russians to withdraw from Ochakov in 1791 foreshadowed continued British anxiety about French control of the Low Countries and the Russian advance in the Black Sea area (31, 5). In February 1793 Britain was drawn into war with revolutionary France. Henceforth Pitt would be expected to provide the kind of war leadership that the nation associated with his father.

When the Revolution began in France in 1789 Pitt, like many of his countrymen, saw no reason to disapprove of the establishment of a constitutional monarchy in France and privately welcomed the internal dissension which could only weaken Britain's most formidable rival. Even when the Revolution became more violent he felt no compulsion to join Austria and Prussia when they went to war with France in 1792. The declaration by the French Convention on 19 November 1792 that they would assist all peoples who wished to 'regain their liberty', an open invitation to revolution, alarmed George III and Burke more than it did Pitt. In the end it was the French who declared war on Britain on 1 February 1793, after the French Ambassador, Chauvelin, had been expelled from London when news was received of the execution of Louis XVI. But the British government had been brought to the point of war when the French showed their disregard for treaties by marching into Belgium and opening the River Scheldt to commerce. Pitt did not intervene against the French Revolution because he disapproved of it but because it had become in a practical way a threat to British interests (54, 93).

The Background

Pitt's war leadership has been sharply criticised by some historians (32) but even his critics have given him credit for two qualities: his dogged persistence in rebuilding the allied coalitions which so frequently crumbled and his complete dominance of the House of Commons. Only a handful of Whigs, associated with Charles James Fox and Charles Grey, stood out against him; for the rest he was the great war leader. For the first half of the nineteenth century men looked back to the clashes between Pitt and Fox as the battle of the giants and felt their successors to be pygmies in comparison. In their different ways, both Canning and Castlereagh were Pitt's disciples and felt themselves to be his heirs.

2 The Age of Canning and Castlereagh

George Canning came from an Anglo-Irish family which had settled in Ulster in the seventeenth century. His father, another George, was disinherited by his father, Stratford Canning,* who disapproved both of his radical views (he had supported John Wilkes) and of his choice of a wife (90). The elder George died when his son was only a year old and in order to support herself and her child his wife, Mary Ann, was forced to go on to the stage, a socially disastrous step which was to be a considerable embarrassment to her famous son later in life, and the subject of many political taunts, but Stratford Canning was prevailed on to send his grandson to Eton. At Eton Canning proved to be both popular and talented, and hesitated whether to make his career in the law or in politics. The law would have been a safer choice for a young man with his way to make in the world but Canning was irresistibly drawn towards politics (45). His success at Eton was repeated at Oxford and in 1792, at the age of twenty-two, he felt sufficiently confident to approach the Tory Prime Minister, William Pitt, for assistance in entering the political world. Canning's background would have made it more natural for him to have entered politics on the Whig side but in 1792 British opinion was already beginning to divide sharply on the subject of the French Revolution. The September massacres disgusted and alarmed many who had previously felt goodwill towards the revolutionary cause and a significant number of Whigs were already moving towards the support of Pitt.

Pitt, who all his life had a talent for attracting the enthusiastic and loyal support of younger men, saw Canning as a promising recruit. He encouraged Canning in his ambitions and a close friendship developed between the two men, so close indeed that it made enemies for Canning among those who were jealous of Pitt's obvious regard for him (45). Pitt found a constituency for him at Newtown in the Isle of Wight and, since this was still in the days of rotten boroughs, he was elected without even seeing his constituency. His early contact with foreign affairs

---

* Not to be confused with another of his grandsons, the famous ambassador of that name.

was fortuitous. The office which Canning really coveted was that of Chief Secretary for Ireland but it was clear that he must first gain some experience in junior office. The office which Pitt found it most convenient to make available to him was that of Under-Secretary at the Foreign Office, under Lord Grenville. Canning was installed at the Foreign Office in January 1796. He quickly found his new job exacting but enthralling. The war with France was at a very delicate stage: the First Coalition was falling to pieces; Prussia had made peace in 1795; Austria made peace at Campo Formio in 1797; even the British made overtures for peace but these came to nothing. Instead, by the beginning of 1799, Britain had drawn Austria, Russia, Naples and Portugal into a new coalition against France. It was a strenuous apprenticeship in diplomacy and Canning had already begun to form his own ideas on policy, although he could not always persuade his chief, Lord Grenville, of their merits. When in March 1799 Pitt transferred him to the India Office he found the work much less interesting.

Canning always had considerable literary talents. Even as an Eton schoolboy he had, with a few like-minded friends, founded a journal, the *Microcosm*, which secured a circulation far beyond Eton and even attracted the attention of George III. Now as a young politician, and with the help of some of the same Eton friends, he produced a new journal, the *Anti-Jacobin*, which was intended to put the government's point of view and to expose as many as possible of what he regarded as the falsehoods of its opponents. 'In effect,' as Wendy Hinde puts it 'the *Anti-Jacobin* tried to do the job that in a modern war would be the responsibility of a ministry of information' **(45)**. And, although it appeared for only a short time, it did it with considerable success.

At the turn of the century Canning's fortunes changed, partly for better, partly for worse. He married an heiress, Joan Scott, the daughter of a Scottish general, thus gaining financial independence which enabled him to purchase a parliamentary seat at Tralee in Ireland. On the other hand William Pitt resigned the premiership because he was unable to persuade George III to agree to extend the franchise to Catholics which Pitt regarded as the necessary concomitant to the Irish Union of 1801. Pitt, like most politicans of his time, had a horror of 'formed opposition' to the king's government and wished to go out alone, feeling that his personal honour was committed but that there was no reason why his political friends should also withdraw: Canning, however, insisted on resigning with him.

Canning returned to office with Pitt in 1804 as Treasurer of the Navy. He was promised cabinet office but before this could be finalised Pitt himself died in January 1806. Pitt's death was a shattering blow to his younger friends and colleagues. In part the blow was a personal one for they had genuinely loved and esteemed their leader, but it was also catastrophic for their careers. Men like Canning had professed few clearly defined principles except loyalty to Pitt, and had looked to him for their political advancement. Canning, however, was out of office for only a comparatively short time until in March 1807 the Duke of Portland formed an administration in which he invited Canning to become Foreign Secretary. This first period at the Foreign Office was to lead to his most spectacular clash with the then Secretary of State for War, Lord Castlereagh.

Castlereagh, one year older than Canning, was also an Ulsterman. He was descended from the English aristocracy through his mother, the daughter of the First Earl of Hertford, but his father's family, the Stewarts, were Scots settlers in Ireland. John Derry describes them as 'tough, hard-working, unromantic Ulstermen, realistic in their approach to the problems confronting them, whether in business or politics', and points out that it was only during Castlereagh's own lifetime that they completed the transition from commerce and provincialism to aristocracy and political power (28). Castlereagh's father had sat in the Irish House of Commons and was raised to the Irish peerage in 1789. Castlereagh himself was educated in Ireland — not at an English public school — although he did go up to the University of Cambridge. He entered the Dublin Parliament as M.P. for County Down in 1790 and was returned to the British Parliament as M.P. for Tregony in Cornwall four years later.

His early career was mainly concerned with his native Ireland. As a young man he had a reputation as a radical who drank toasts to George Washington, the success of the French Revolution and 'our sovereign lord the people', but in 1791 he visited France and Belgium and was disillusioned by what he saw of the Revolution. He still sympathised with some aspects of it but he doubted the revolutionaries' ability to control the forces they had unleashed. The 1790s were a troubled decade in Ireland, particularly after the outbreak of the war in 1793; by 1796 he was helping to restore order in the north. From the beginning he had distinguished between his attitude to Irish and to British politics. In Ireland he regarded himself as a Whig, firmly opposed to the corrupt Dublin establishment at 'the Castle', but even before he became a British M.P. he had publicly declared his support for Pitt. Although an admirer of Pitt, Castlereagh was not as a young man in Pitt's intimate circle as Canning was, but he had enough influential friends in England, mainly connections of his mother's family, to bring him rapid advancement in public life. In 1797 he became a member of the Privy Council and the following year Chief Secretary for Ireland, and was thus Chief Secretary during the Irish rising of 1798. He was to be hated by sections of both Catholic and Protestant opinion for his part in the suppression of the rebellion and the eloquent foes he made at that time were to dog him throughout his life and even after his death. Byron apostrophized him

> Cold-blooded, smooth-faced, placid miscreant!
> Dabbling its sleek young hands in Erin's gore.

More sober historical research has suggested that Castlereagh understood the underlying discontents in Ireland very well and, as far as was consistent with the restoration of order (the rebellion after all took place during a dangerous foreign war), tried to reduce severity to a minimum (28). The rebellion brought to the fore the long-term question of Ireland. Castlereagh aligned himself with those who saw the only solution as the parliamentary union of Britain and Ireland. He was assailed for treachery to Ireland and a complete abandonment of his earlier views but his opinion was in fact partly formed by his belief that the Dublin Parliament was irredeemably corrupt. Like Pitt he believed that Union must be accompanied by Catholic emancipation.

Unlike Canning, however, he took Pitt's advice that there was no need for his political friends to go out with him and in July 1802 he became President of the Board of Control for India in the Addington administration. In July 1805, during Pitt's last administration, he added the Secretaryship for War and the Colonies to the Presidency of the Board of Control. Like Canning he was out of office immediately after Pitt's death but joined the Portland administration, again as Secretary for War and the Colonies.

When Portland's ministry came into power the outlook in Europe was once again very black. The Third Coalition of Britain, Russia and Austria, formed during Pitt's last administration, had crumbled: the Austrians had been crushed at Austerlitz in December 1805; the Prussians who, although not members of the Third Coalition, had subsequently re-entered the war, were decisively defeated at Jena and Auerstädt in October 1806; the Tsar Alexander chose to come to terms with Napoleon at Tilsit in July 1807. The Treaty of Tilsit divided the hegemony of Europe between France and Russia with the balance in favour of France. Russia recognised the subject states which Napoleon had set up in Italy, Holland and Germany and Alexander was to offer his mediation between France and Britain. So much the British knew from the open clauses of the treaty but they guessed that there were secret clauses too; they suspected a threat to their Indian empire because the French had encouraged the Russians in their conflicts with Turkey and their ambitions in the Near East. More immediately, Alexander and Napoleon had agreed that if the British did not accept Russian mediation at once Russia would make common cause with France against her. Denmark, Sweden and Portugal were all to be involved against Britain. The Continental System was to be tightened.

The Continental System was the French reply to the one great victory that Britain had won in those years, that of Trafalgar in October 1805. Trafalgar had confirmed Britain in command of the seas and forced Napoleon to shelve his invasion plans. Instead Napoleon had tried to blockade Britain by administrative decree. The Berlin Decrees of November 1806 closed all French ports and those of her allies and satellites to any ship coming from Britain or her colonies. Britain retaliated by the Order in Council of January 1807 which forbade neutrals to trade with those ports from which the British were excluded. The British hoped that the obloquy for these measures would fall on Napoleon, but in fact – although the system was widely evaded by extensive smuggling – the British were the more unpopular with neutrals. Their command of the seas enabled them to stop, search and, if anything that fell under their strict definition of contraband was found, confiscate foreign ships. The British definition of 'maritime rights' was to be indignantly challenged by many European powers, as well as by the United States [doc. 12].

The British did not know the exact terms of the secret clauses of the Treaty of Tilsit but aided by still mysterious intelligence work (45, 91) they guessed them fairly accurately. They persuaded the Portuguese royal family to flee to their colony of Brazil and to surrender the Portuguese fleet to Britain. The Danes were less amenable and in September 1808 a British expedition bombarded Copenhagen until the Danes agreed to give up their fleet. The British public were less convinced than the government of the likelihood of Danish hostility and the government's action was severely criticised in many quarters; Canning himself confessed to having spent some sleepless nights (45).

Fears arising from the Treaty of Tilsit not only led the British into some spectacular gunboat diplomacy, they also helped to initiate the strong British interest in the Iberian Peninsula which lasted throughout the Napoleonic Wars and well into the nineteenth century. Britain was encouraged to active intervention not only by her traditional alliance with Portugal, dating back to the Middle Ages, but also by the resistance movements against the French invaders which appeared in northern Spain and made a direct appeal for British assistance in 1808. Canning was later to claim that his response to these requests was due to a genuine response to the claims of Spanish nationalism [doc. 7] and unlike Pitt or Castlereagh, he appreciated the importance of nationalism in the struggle against Napoleon from an early date (80, 90). In fact his response was cautious – not surprisingly as the various Spanish groups found it very difficult to co-operate (45) and British fortunes in the Peninsula fluctuated considerably at first. Sir Arthur Wellesley, later Duke of Wellington, decisively defeated the French general, Junot, at Vimiero in August 1808 but the victory was thrown away by the Convention of Cintra which not only allowed the defeated French army to withdraw, with no undertaking that they would not return to fight in the Peninsula, but actually provided British ships to convey them back to France. The British commander-in-chief, Dalrymple, was recalled but the government, especially Castlereagh at the War Office and Canning at the Foreign Office were strongly criticised.

Even worse from the government's point of view was the ill-fated Walcheren expedition, intended to capture the key port of Antwerp. Partly due to the shortcomings of the commander, Lord Chatham, the Younger Pitt's elder brother, Antwerp was not captured and the British expedition suffered serious casualties, more from disease than from enemy action.

The Secretary of State for War, Castlereagh, began to seem politically expendable. This may well have been unfair to Castlereagh; historians have generally concluded that he was a good Secretary of State for War, with a wide grasp of the strategic essentials of the war, who did a great deal to remedy the chaotic organisation of the War Office (28). He was certainly not alone responsible for the appointment of unsuitable commanders like Lord Chatham. Criticisms of his conduct of the war became merged however with cabinet intrigues to find a replacement as Prime Minister for the Duke of Portland whose health was failing. When Castlereagh learnt of these intrigues, he jumped to the conclusion that Canning was at the bottom of them. He challenged Canning to a duel which was fought on Putney Heath on 21 September 1809; he escaped unscathed but Canning was slightly wounded in the leg. Although duels were not unknown in Regency England, one between two Cabinet ministers caused something of a sensation; both men returned to the back benches and the amiable, and not untalented, Spencer Perceval succeeded Portland as Prime Minister.

Castlereagh returned to office in February 1812 as Foreign Secretary. After Perceval's assassination in May he continued as Foreign Secretary under Lord Liverpool, combining it with the Leadership of the House of

Commons. This placed an enormous double burden on Castlereagh. As Leader of the House he was responsible for the defence of much of the government's domestic legislation, more particularly because most of the senior ministers sat in the Lords and Liverpool's cabinet team in the Commons was weak. (Lord Castlereagh as an Irish peer did not, of course, sit in the Lords even when he succeeded his father as Marquess of Londonderry in 1821.) He had also to run the Foreign Office during the critical years of Napoleon's defeat.

The first priority in 1812 was clearly the conduct of the war. The whole war situation was soon to be changed by Napoleon's invasion of Russia in June 1812 but it was not at first apparent how disastrous this would be for Napoleon. The Liverpool administration continued to give Wellington firm backing in the Peninsula and they reaped their reward when Wellington won a major victory at Vitoria in June 1813 and at last a British army stood ready to invade France.

Less happy from the British point of view was the war with the United States which broke out in June 1812. The immediate cause of the war was the British interpretation of maritime rights, including the right of blockade, which she was enforcing in her struggle with Napoleon's Continental System, but there were other issues in the background. The Americans were sensitive about their colonial past and quick to suspect that the British still treated them as inferiors and did not accord them full nation status. They resented the continued existence of the British colony of Canada on North American soil and suspected that the British were now encouraging their Spanish allies in their still extensive claims in Florida and elsewhere on the North American continent. The war was essentially a stalemate; although not without stirring incidents, long remembered on both sides. The Americans burnt Toronto. The British burnt the President's residence (not yet called the White House, it was white-washed to hide the signs of the British attack). The *Shannon* and the *Chesapeake* fought in Massachusetts Bay and became the subject of a scurrilous, and very popular, British ballad. But neither side could hope to gain much from the war.

As long ago as 1783 the Prime Minister, Lord Shelburne, and his young Chancellor of the Exchequer, William Pitt, had believed that despite their political estrangement the economies of the two countries were naturally complementary and should be linked in a common trading system. Pitt had never forgotten the ideal and had tried to realise it, notably at the time of the Jay Treaty in 1794. Ironically, the British Orders-in-Council so far as they related to the United States were abrogated almost the week the war broke out, and the merchant interests in America, especially in New England, who had been successfully evading the Orders in any case, never favoured the war. Castlereagh, in this as in so much else the pupil of Pitt, was determinedly conciliatory when the time came to make peace in 1814. In particular, he was careful to give full recognition to American nationhood. But the peace treaty, signed at Ghent, left most of the real issues between the two countries blurred. The exact frontiers between the United States and British North America were not defined in important areas which were only just being explored. Fishery disputes remained. Castlereagh deliberately left the whole question of maritime rights off the agenda for the settlement; with the ending of the war in Europe the matter was no longer so urgent (71).

For the British government the situation in Europe was much more important than their relations with the United States. Here too Castlereagh still had Pitt's policy to guide him. In 1805, in response to Russian overtures, Pitt had sketched out a blue-print for a possible settlement [doc. 10]. Castlereagh could not, and did not attempt to follow it in every detail [doc. 11] – the situation had changed in many ways since 1805 – but it has long been accepted by historians that it was his starting point (93). Pitt had wanted to free the countries France had subjugated and reduce France to her former limits, provide effective barriers against future French aggression, and come to some general agreement with the other powers to guarantee the system. How exactly this was to be done depended on how completely France was defeated. Austria did not want the former Austrian Netherlands (Belgium) returned to her and Pitt was already considering an enlarged Holland which would control at least Antwerp. If Italy were freed from French control it would have to be reorganised and Pitt favoured an enlarged Piedmont and an increase in Austrian influence. Germany could not return to the over 300 separate states which had existed there before the Napoleonic wars: it too would have to be grouped in larger units with Austrian power predominant in the south, Prussian in the north. A 'balance' between Austrian and Prussian interests was necessary in the first place to encourage both to continue the struggle against Napoleon. Pitt declined to discuss the future of the Ottoman empire but showed willingness to use Britain's numerous colonial conquests during the war as bargaining counters in European issues. Through all the complications of the formation of the final Coalition against Napoleon these remained roughly Britain's objectives.

Even after Napoleon had suffered severe reverses in Russia, it was extremely difficult to persuade all the great, and some of the minor, powers of Europe to remain consistent in their opposition to France. There was always the danger that powers would make a separate peace as they had done before. The British role was, as it had been throughout the war, a diplomatic and financial one, rather than a military one, although she now at last had a sizeable army on the continent, under Wellington in Spain. The British had the advantage of a comparatively sophisticated banking and commercial system and the great potential of their industrial revolution behind them, despite the very real and widespread economic distress in Britain especially in the years 1811–12, which was a direct consequence of the war and the Continental System. The actual raising of the war loans was a complicated business and names which were to be famous later in the century began to be heard. Nathan Rothschild, for example, played an important part in supplying the ready cash (99, 43).

Russia and Prussia signed an alliance against Napoleon at Kalisch on 27 February 1813. The Swedes, encouraged by a sudsidy treaty from Britain, joined them a month later. The allies at first fared badly against the French who won victories at Lützen and Bautzen in May 1813. Napoleon's folly in agreeing to the Armistice of Pleswitz the following month, however, not only gave them a chance to regroup militarily but also to win over the Austrians. Metternich, who was now the Austrian Chancellor, conducted the negotiations with skill and ultimately, from the Austrian point of view, success. Austria was bound to France by dynastic ties through Napoleon's marriage to Marie-Louise, the daughter of the Emperor Francis I of Austria, but what weighed more with Metternich was the fear that the defeat of France would increase the power of Austria's own rivals, Russia and Prussia. Ideally, he wished to see a Europe in which the French and the Russians balanced one another and Prussia was not allowed to take the lead in Germany at Austria's expense (57). The Austrians joined the Russians and the Prussians by the Treaty of Reichenbach of 27 June 1813. The allied cause was almost lost when the Austrian general, Schwarzenberg, prematurely engaged the French at Dresden in August 1813 and suffered a severe defeat, but Dresden was negated two months later when the allied armies defeated Napoleon at the battle of Leipzig [doc. 35]. Meanwhile negotiations about the forthcoming peace continued between the continental allies and fresh terms were agreed between them at Teplitz and Ried in September–October 1813.

Although the continental powers were more inclined to take Britain seriously as a military power after the battle of Vitoria they had shown a, from the British point of view alarming, tendency to ignore her during the negotiations in the summer and early autumn of 1813, informing her late, if at all, of their intentions (99). Indeed, the British diplomatic service in Europe had almost fallen to pieces during the period of Napoleon's supremacy and even physical communication and the passage of news between Britain and the continental allies was difficult until allied successes began to free some of the ports of western and northern Europe from Napoleonic control (28). The two most important British representatives in Europe at this time were Castlereagh's own step-brother, Charles Stewart, the Ambassador to Prussia, and Lord Cathcart, the Ambassador to Russia. In August 1813 Castlereagh sent out a third man to join these, the Fourth Earl of Aberdeen (see chapter 4), who was to be Ambassador to Austria. Castlereagh has been much criticised for his choice on the grounds of Aberdeen's youth and inexperience and imperfect command of French (99), but protocol demanded an aristocrat rather than a career diplomat — even if career diplomats had not been in very short supply in 1813. It was true that Aberdeen was only twenty-nine but he had travelled widely and it was a young man's world. Castlereagh himself had been Chief Secretary for Ireland at the age of twenty-eight and Canning had been Foreign Secretary at thirty-seven. Aberdeen undoubtedly spoke some French — he had studied the language while living in France during the Peace of Amiens — but it is true that his lack of fluency and still more his general lack of diplomatic experience did enable the continental diplomats to overreach him. The situation was not helped by the distrust and jealousy that developed between Stewart, Cathcart and Aberdeen (36) and the fact that Castlereagh could only give contingent instructions when the military situation was still uncertain and it was quite possible that the new Coalition might collapse like its predecessors.

On 18 September 1813 Castlereagh sent Cathcart an important despatch [doc. 11] outlining the terms Britain would like to see embodied in a peace treaty. He also alluded to the possibility of a continuing alliance of Britain, Russia, Prussia, Austria and Sweden, and possibly Spain, Portugal and Sicily, to protect the continent against further French aggression. This can be seen either as a development of Pitt's suggestions of 1805 or perhaps simply as an attempt to ensure that Britain would not be left out of negotiations as she had been in the summer of 1813. Cathcart received the despatch on 18 October.

After the battle of Leipzig on 19 October, the centre of negotiations moved to Frankfurt, and a negotiated peace with Napoleon now seemed possible. Metternich took the lead in these negotiations and Aberdeen alone of the British diplomats was in his confidence. Aberdeen incautiously agreed to allow freedom of trade and navigation (*la liberté du commerce et de la navigation*) to be one of the bases for discussion; he also agreed that the discussions should proceed on the basis of France retaining the 'natural frontiers' of the Alps, the Rhine and the Pyrenees. Neither proposal was acceptable to Castlereagh, who was determined that 'maritime rights' should not be smuggled into the negotiations [doc. 12] and unwilling to agree to any frontier which would leave France in control of Antwerp. It had, however, always been accepted that the final French frontiers would ultimately depend on the fortunes of war, as would the question of whether Napoleon was to retain the French throne or be displaced, and Napoleon was far from beaten after Leipzig. Although he was fighting with a new and virtually untrained army, he won a number of victories in the winter of 1813–14 (99).

To conduct policy from London in a rapidly changing situation was clearly difficult and in December 1813, with the consent of his Cabinet colleagues, Castlereagh took the unusual step of going to the continent to take part in the negotiations himself. From the time of his arrival he was remarkably successful in making the British voice count. He played a leading part in summoning a conference at Chatillon in February 1814 and on 1 March he secured the Treaty of Chaumont [doc. 2] by which Britain, Austria, Prussia and Russia bound themselves not to make a separate peace with Napoleon. But, more than this, in return for substantial British subsidies, the other powers engaged themselves to guarantee the territorial settlement to be made at the peace for twenty years. This was the real beginning of the Congress System (96, 99).

On 31 March the allied armies entered Paris. A few days later Napoleon abdicated. Peace negotiations could now begin in earnest. A treaty, the First Treaty of Paris, was quickly concluded with France, where Louis XVIII, the brother of the executed Louis XVI, had been restored to the throne. France was to be restricted to the frontiers of 1792 with some minor modifications; she surrendered her claims to the territory she had conquered in Germany, Italy, Switzerland and the Low Countries. Much of the map of Europe would have to be redrawn and it was provided that the final settlement should be made at a Congress of all the Powers involved, including France, to be held at Vienna. There was no question of excluding France as Germany was excluded from the Paris Peace Conference in 1919 because the other powers wished to emphasise that, with the restoration of Louis XVIII, legitimate authority and normal relations with other powers had returned to the French government.

The Congress of Vienna met on 1 November 1814 but its proceedings were dilatory, although conducted against a background of great social glitter leading to the famous quip 'Le Congrès danse, mais il ne marche pas' (68). It was rudely interrupted in March 1815 by the return of Napoleon from his initial exile in Elba. After the defeat of Napoleon at Waterloo in June a second Treaty of Paris was imposed, with harsher terms than those of the earlier treaty. France was now compelled to return the many art treasures which had been looted during the Napoleonic wars and which, surprisingly, she had been allowed to retain by the first treaty. French frontiers were further restricted to the limits of 1789, again with some minor modifications. France was now to pay a war indemnity of 700 million francs and allow the allies to garrison her frontier fortresses for five years. The terms were still moderate because the allies still wished to spare the restored Bourbon dynasty any humiliation, but it was all too obvious that Louis XVIII had come back 'in the baggage train of the allies' and that many Frenchmen were still loyal to Napoleon. The spectre of 'Bonapartism' was to haunt not only French governments but also European diplomacy for another half century.

Meanwhile the Vienna Congress had continued. It was what in modern terms would be called a 'summit conference'. The Emperor of Austria, with Metternich at his elbow, was the host. The Tsar of Russia was there, accompanied by his Foreign Secretary, Count Nesselrode, who was to be an important figure in European diplomacy until 1856. King Frederick William III of Prussia was accompanied by Hardenberg and Stein, who had played such an important part in the revival of Prussia and her reassertion of great power status. The astute and experienced Talleyrand represented France and was soon to be able to exploit the divisions between the former allies to his country's advantage. Although the decisions of the Congress were to be dominated by the great powers, every state of Christian Europe, including the Papacy, was represented. The Turks, not being Christians, were the only notable absentees. At first Castlereagh himself represented Britain but in February 1815 he was compelled to return to London to deal with home affairs (he was still leader of the House of Commons) and leave British representation to the Duke of Wellington. Wellington enjoyed enormous prestige on the continent but Castlereagh left the Congress reluctantly feeling, probably rightly (28), that he had won the confidence of the other delegates and that, particularly considering that he had comparatively few substantial cards in his hand, he had been remarkably successful in securing British aims.

The most tendentious question before the Congress was the fate of Poland and Saxony (96). Over the previous forty or so years Poland had been first partitioned by Russia, Prussia and Austria and then partially reconstituted by Napoleon as the Grand Duchy of Warsaw. The Tsar Alexander would have like to have seen a restored Poland given into

Russian keeping. The British government was sorry that the question was on the agenda of the Congress at all and they were aware that the fate of Poland aroused public interest in Britain [doc. 14]. The Prussians wished to claim the whole of Saxony, whose king had been caught fighting on the wrong side at the end of the war. Castlereagh's attitude was influenced by his deep distrust of Russian policy. Alexander was already showing signs of the instability which made him the support of liberalism one day and of reaction the next and Castlereagh feared his ambitions both in the East and in Europe. Generally, Castlereagh felt that Britain's policy approximated most closely to that of Austria: both desired a moderate policy towards France and the establishment of a 'balance' on the continent, particularly between French and Russian power; both were agreed that the allies should content themselves with the territory they had held in 1805, or its equivalent [doc. 11]. Castlereagh, however, was not wholly adverse to Prussia acquiring Saxony. He saw Prussia also as an important counterpoise to France. He looked back to a proposal made by Pitt in 1806 to encourage Prussia to establish herself on the Rhine to check future French aggressions, although he was aware that there were some dangers in such a plan [doc 13]. Austria, however, was reluctant to see Prussia in control of Saxony.

In November 1814 Russia and Prussia made common cause and on 3 January 1815 Britain, Austria and France made a defensive alliance, later joined by some of the smaller powers. The French army was partially mobilised. Faced with this determination, the Russians and the Prussians compromised: the Tsar was to become king of a large part, although not the whole of pre-partition Poland, with Warsaw as its capital; vague promises of representative institutions were held out to the Poles [doc. 15]; Prussia contented herself with part of Saxony but gained important territories in the Rhineland. The Prussians accepted the Rhineland (which was Catholic in religion and more sophisticated politically than most Prussian territories) without enthusiasm but her assumption, however reluctantly, of Austria's traditional role as the defender of Germany against France played an important part in her ability during the next fifty years to wrest the leadership of Germany from Austria. This was not apparent in 1815. Bavaria was re-established as a powerful state with ties of interest with Austria. Hanover, of which the British King was still the Elector, received additional territory. Altogether thirty-nine German states (in contrast to the three hundred German states of pre-war days) joined together in a German Confederation, of which Austria retained the presidency [doc. 15].

Austria took some compensation for Prussia's territorial gains in

Italy. Lombardy, as well as the former Venetian Republic, was to be under direct Austrian rule. Austrian influence was strong in Tuscany and Modena, both ruled by Austrian Dukes, and in Parma and Piacenza, which had been given to the Empress Marie-Louise, Napoleon's Austrian wife. The Congress restored Naples and Sicily to the Bourbon, Ferdinand I, who entered into treaty relations with Austria to align his policy with hers. King Victor Emmanuel I was restored to Piedmont-Sardinia which was strengthened by the addition of Genoa. The Pope regained control of the Papal States [doc. 15] .

Austria had declined to take back the old Austrian Netherlands and these were now united with Holland under the House of Orange; this too was intended to strengthen states which neighboured France. It also satisfied the British by ensuring that no great power controlled the Low Countries (77) [doc. 15] .

Comparing the terms of the Treaty of Vienna of 9 June 1815 with Castlereagh's instructions to Cathcart of 18 September 1813 [docs. 11, 15] , it is possible to see that in general terms Britain had secured the European settlement she wanted. Castlereagh had also persuaded the Congress to condemn the Atlantic Slave Trade, which Britain had declared illegal for her own subjects in 1807, although no machinery was provided for its suppression and its abolition in practice remained a problem for British foreign policy until the American Civil War. Castlereagh, like Pitt, held a possibly exaggerated view of the leverage which could be exerted from the fact that during the war Britain had captured most French and Dutch colonies and some territories belonging to Spain and Portugal (93). Russia, Prussia and Austria in fact cared little about overseas questions and Britain had virtually a free hand in arranging matters here. Strategic considerations, rather than immediate profitability, seem to have been the deciding factor in almost every case. Britain kept the Cape of Good Hope and Ceylon, taken from the Dutch, Heligoland, which had been Danish, Malta, formerly belonging to the Knights of St John, and the Ionian Islands and Mauritius, previously in French hands; in the West Indies they kept Trinidad from Spain and Tobago from the French. But they returned Martinique and Guadeloupe (technically in Swedish hands at the end of the war), both important sugar islands, the Isle of Bourbon and French Guiana (then in Portuguese hands) to France; and then returned the very lucrative Dutch East Indies, including Java, to Holland.

The Treaty of Vienna, together with the First and Second Treaties of Paris of 30 May 1814 and 20 November 1815 respectively, embodied the peace settlements at the end of the Napoleonic wars which constituted 'normality' in Europe for over half a century. As late as 1863 Lord Palmerston was to resist strongly any suggestion that they were no longer valid and the basis of the organisation of Europe [doc. 58]. While the Congress was still sitting Napoleon's 'Hundred Days' had forcibly reminded the allies that they must be prepared to defend the settlement against future French encroachments and on the same day that the Second Treaty of Paris was signed, Britain, Austria, Russia and Prussia joined together in the Quadruple Alliance by which they agreed to uphold the settlement and to confer together as occasion might require [doc. 3]. This gave substance to the vaguer promise made in the Treaty of Chaumont and brought the Congress System proper into being. Two months earlier the Tsar had persuaded most European Heads of State to subscribe to a much more mystical form of European union, the Holy Alliance [doc. 4]. The British politely pleaded constitutional difficulties to avoid signing. Castlereagh's commitment was entirely to the more down to earth Congress System, the purpose of which he saw as strictly limited to the prevention of a French disruption of the peace settlement.

The first Congress to meet under the 1815 arrangements assembled at Aix-la-Chapelle in the autumn of 1818 (68). The Tsar Alexander I of Russia, the Emperor Francis I of Austria and King Frederick William III of Prussia again attended in person; Castlereagh and Wellington again represented Britain. The business of the meeting was fairly harmonious. The French government of Louis XVIII was anxious to see the occupation troops removed so that France could once again be regarded as a normal monarchical state. The other four powers were prepared to agree to this and signed a new Quintuple Alliance including France, although the original Quadruple Alliance, aimed at checking France, was also renewed. Alexander was anxious that the powers should sign a strong declaration against all revolutionary movements. More particularly, he wanted the allies to intervene to help the King of Spain regain his South American empire, where most of the former Spanish colonies had declared their independence. Castlereagh was strongly opposed to the last suggestion and both he and Metternich distrusted Alexander's motives for the first. Alexander was fobbed off with a general declaration of moral solidarity.

The next Congress, which met at Troppau in Bohemia (Opava in modern Czechoslovakia) in October 1820, was confronted by more immediate dangers to the 1815 settlement. A revolution in Spain had compelled the restored King Ferdinand VII to accept the constitution drawn up by the Cortes in 1812 which, modelled as it was on the French constitution of 1791, was regarded by contemporaries as ultra-democratic. Ferdinand I was confronted by a similar rising in Naples. The Troppau Congress was called by the Tsar and attended by Prussian and Austrian representatives but not by Britain and France. The three Eastern Powers signed a document, which has become known to history as the Troppau Protocol [doc. 18], in which they committed themselves to intervene if revolutionary changes in any state seemed to threaten any other state (98).

Castlereagh dissociated himself from any such sentiments. He had already set out the British position in what Professor Temperley once called 'the most famous State Paper in British history' (93), that of 5 May 1820 [doc. 19]. He made it clear that he believed Britain's obligations to be limited to guaranteeing the territorial arrangements of the Vienna Settlement for twenty years and preventing the return of Napoleon's dynasty to France. The Spanish revolution was an internal matter for Spain and he could not justify intervention to the British public. If actual danger threatened the European system England would 'be found in our place' but 'this Country cannot, and will not, act upon abstract and speculative Principles of Precaution'. He repeated these views in a circular despatch to all the major British envoys abroad after the issue of the Troppau Protocol. The despatch was published at the time, January 1821, and extracts from the State Paper were published early in 1823.

The Troppau meeting was adjourned to Laibach (Ljubljana in modern Yugoslavia), where it reassembled in January 1821. This time Britain was represented at the meeting by the British Ambassador in Vienna, Castlereagh's brother, now Lord Stewart. Ferdinand of Naples appealed to the Congress for help. In view of Austria's treaty agreements with Naples, the British could not object to the despatch of an Austrian army but they strongly opposed the use of any international force. While the Congress was still sitting news was received of a revolt in Wallachia and Moldavia (part of modern Romania) which preceded the main Greek revolt in the Morea against their Turkish overlords. This had the effect of once again uniting British and Austrian policy as both were anxious that the Russians should not profit by the situation to gain further territory at the expense of Turkey. The Tsar was divided in his mind. He did not wish to support rebels, but the Sultan of Turkey was not a Christian sovereign and Alexander was to some extent influenced by Panslavist ideals, seeing Russia as the natural protector of the Christian peoples of the Balkans against the Muslims. He was glad enough to agree with Metternich that there should be no European intervention at this stage (98).

Laibach had settled very little and a new Congress was arranged to meet at Verona in 1822. Castlereagh originally intended to be present himself but before it met he was dead. For ten strenuous years he had carried the almost impossible double burden of Leader of the House of Commons and Foreign Secretary. He had no illusions about his own unpopularity in radical circles at Home and it is possible that the breaking point was reached when he feared that he was being framed for a homosexual offence by his enemies (28). Although his friends recognised that his mind was giving way, they were unable to prevent him from taking his own life by plunging a penknife into his throat.

His successor at the Foreign Office was George Canning. Canning had had a less successful career than Castlereagh since they had both resigned in 1809. He could have become Foreign Secretary in July 1812 but he was unwilling to serve under Castlereagh as Leader of the House of Commons. In 1814 Lord Liverpool, an old and close friend of Canning, had suggested that he might go as British Minister to Lisbon to greet the Portuguese royal family on their return from their exile in Brazil. In fact the Portuguese royal family delayed their return but Canning spent rather over a year in Lisbon. From June 1816 to December 1820 he sat in the Cabinet as President of the Board of Control for India, not then a very prestigious office (45), but it brought him into contact once again with foreign policy. Outwardly at least Canning and Castlereagh had made up their differences and Canning was able to exercise some influence on Castlereagh's policy. It is possible that he had some hand in the famous State Paper of May 1820 and certainly, on coming back into office, he publicly accepted it as the basis of his own policy (91, 93). He also adopted Castlereagh's draft instructions for the British delegation at the Congress of Verona.

When Castlereagh died so unexpectedly, Canning was about to depart to become Governor-General of India, but the position he had always wanted was that of Foreign Secretary and he spent some anxious weeks wondering whether it would be offered to him and whether he should accept it, if it was (45). Professor Temperley long ago advanced the thesis that Canning's main work at the Foreign Office was to destroy the 'Neo-Holy Alliance' (90, 91), the perversion of the Quintuple Alliance to crush revolution, or even moderate change, wherever it manifested itself in Europe. Later historians have tended to see Canning's policy in more pragmatic terms (45).

When he resumed the Foreign Office the three main problems were the fate of Spain and her colonies, the stability of Portugal and the Eastern Question. At Verona the Tsar again urged the desirability of international intervention in Spain, and perhaps in Italy too; he even offered to station a Russian army in Piedmont to be ready for such an intervention. The presence of a Russian army in western Europe was as unwelcome to the other great powers, especially Austria, as it was to Britain and the Tsar was dissuaded. The British, now represented at Verona by the Duke of Wellington, also argued against a unilateral French intervention in Spain, but here they were less successful. After the failure of an attempted countercoup by Ferdinand VII a French army marched into Spain in April 1823 and, contrary to Wellington's predictions, found no difficulty in subduing the country. Autocracy was restored.

The main question for Britain now was the fate of Spain's American colonies. The United States had already recognised the independence of Colombia and Mexico in 1822 and of the United Provinces of La Plata (Argentina) and Chile in January 1823. British interest in South America was entirely commercial: financial and trading links were becoming increasingly strong. South America is one of the classic illustrations of the fact that no government of a trading nation like Britain could afford to ignore mercantile interests but, equally, it illustrates that even in the 1820s the British government was seeking the 'Open Door' for commerce and was anxious neither to seek special privileges nor take on extended commitments (72). Canning moved very cautiously. At home he had to take account of the opposition of the King, George IV – an old enemy of his on domestic questions – and of Wellington, neither of whom wished to recognise republics created by rebellions. The most immediate problem was to prevent outside interference. The eastern powers might wish to intervene but none of them had the necessary naval resources. It would, however, have been possible for France to have sent a fleet to reassert Spanish claims.

Canning brought sufficient diplomatic pressure to bear on the French for them to agree, through their Ambassador in London, the Prince de Polignac, that French intervention in Spain should not be extended to the colonies. The agreement was embodied in a document known as the Polignac Memorandum [doc. 20]. Canning also opened negotiations with the United States with a view to a joint declaration against any foreign intervention in the former Spanish colonies. The United States government hesitated but Anglo-American relations were still strained and they opted instead for unilateral action in the declaration, known to history as the Monroe Doctrine, affirming that the American continent was no longer open to European colonisation. The Americans may have been influenced by the fact that the Tsar had just issued a *ukase*, claiming wide territories in the north-east of the continent but it was also potentially anti-British in that the territorial claims of the United States and of British North America were not yet settled. The British were indignant too because they were well aware that it would be the British navy which would, in practice, stand between Latin America and intervention. Canning took the unusual steps, not only of circulating the Polignac Memorandum to British embassies abroad, but also of making it public by laying it before Parliament so that the world in general, and South Americans in particular, could see that it antedated the Monroe Doctrine. There remained the question of the actual recognition of independent states in Latin America and here Canning still moved cautiously, refusing to act until he had sent out special envoys to make sure that the states were viable and firmly established. In the end he only initially recognised Mexico, Argentina and Colombia (100).

Portugal was a problem to Britain throughout the 1820s and 1830s. Canning, who had strongly opposed the idea of outside intervention in Spain and Italy, felt remarkably free to intervene in Portugal. His justification was always that he acted to forestall intervention by other powers, an action which perhaps led to Talleyrand's witticism that 'non-intervention was a word signifying much the same as intervention'. Canning could argue that Portugal had a 'special relationship' with Britain dating back to the Middle Ages and that since the seventeenth century Britain had been pledged to help Portugal against foreign attacks and had honoured that pledge several times in the eighteenth century. Portugal also held a special place in British interest and affections because of the Peninsular campaigns during the Napoleonic wars.

King John VI finally returned from his Brazilian exile in July 1821, leaving his son Pedro as Regent of Brazil. On his return John accepted a constitution but the absolutists who disliked the constitution found a leader in John's younger son, Miguel. Canning forestalled a *coup d'état* by Miguel by sending a British fleet to Lisbon, on which John took refuge until Miguel was expelled from Portugal in 1824. Meanwhile Brazil, which had been the centre of the government of the Portuguese empire from 1807 to 1821, refused to return to a subordinate colonial status. John, encouraged by Canning, recognised Brazil as an independent state with Pedro as its first emperor in 1825. This solution, however, caused problems when John himself died the following year. Pedro renounced his claims to the Portuguese throne in favour of his seven-year-old daughter, Donna Maria Gloria; to make her succession more popular he granted a new liberal constitution, the 'Charter', to replace the previous one which had been largely abrogated during the struggles of 1823. The absolutists, led by the army, once again asserted Miguel's claim to the throne. This time Canning went even further along the path of intervention and, not long before his own death in 1827, despatched 5,000 British troops to ensure Maria's succession and the acceptance of the Charter.

Britain was interested in the fate of the Iberian Peninsula, partly because of its close ties with South and Central America, partly because of its intrinsic strategic importance at the western end of the Mediterranean. She was becoming equally interested in the fate of the Ottoman empire at the opposite end of the Mediterranean. That empire's weakness had begun to be revealed to the world by Russian successes during the reign of Catherine the Great: Napoleon's Egyptian campaign and the Treaty of Tilsit had awakened British fears for the security of her Indian empire. Long before the Suez Canal was opened in 1869, the British were determined not to see a rival great power dominant in the eastern Mediterranean or in command of the land routes across Asia Minor and down the Euphrates Valley. The capital of the Ottoman empire, Constantinople, was the greatest political and strategic prize of all (49, 92).

The Greek revolt which began in 1821 continued until 1830. It aroused mixed feelings in London, as it had done in St Petersburg, although for very different reasons. On the one hand, it was dangerous because it presented a threat to the stability of the Ottoman empire and from the time of Pitt the British government had believed that the preservation of the Ottoman empire offered the best hope of stability in the region (31). On the other hand, there was a good deal of sympathy for the Greeks among the educated classes who had been nurtured on the classics. Philhellenic societies were founded in both Britain and France. Lord Byron, who was to die in Greece in April 1824, was their best known propagandist. It was difficult for any government to support the Muslim Turks against the Christian Greeks. News of Turkish atrocities (although there were Greek atrocities too) further excited public feeling.

Canning felt some personal sympathy for the Greeks but his policy was essentially guided by his calculation of British interests. In March 1823 he recognised the Greeks as belligerents – previously their status had merely been that of 'rebels'. Alexander tried first to get the British to agree to a joint intervention and then to summon a conference of all the European great powers. Canning refused to agree to the first and withdrew his support for the second in January 1824 (45). Meanwhile things were going badly for the Greeks. The Sultan had called on Ibrahim, the heir and adopted son of Mehemet Ali, the energetic Pasha (Governor) of Egypt, for assistance. Ibrahim was one of the ablest soldiers of the time and, having first secured Crete, he mounted an almost entirely successful campaign against mainland Greece in the spring of 1825; thousands were killed and it was rumoured that Ibrahim intended to repopulate the country with reliable Muslims from Egypt and Africa (27).

In December 1825 Alexander died. His heir, Nicholas I, was an unknown quantity in the West and even his right to the succession had been in some doubt. He soon revealed himself to be a staunch autocrat, but he was prepared to negotiate unilaterally with Britain on Greece. He was much less committed to Congress diplomacy than Alexander and this suited Canning very well. Wellington was sent to St Petersburg and the result was the Protocol of St Petersburg, signed in April 1826, by which the two powers agreed that Greece should become an autonomous state, although still paying tribute to the Ottoman empire [doc. 22]. The Protocol did not find favour with Metternich but France was prepared to become a party to it and by the Treaty of London of July 1827 Britain, France and Russia agreed to what was virtually an armed mediation to compel the Turks to accept it. Their fleets in the eastern Mediterranean were authorised to blockade Ibrahim's army. This led to the almost accidental battle of Navarino on 20 October 1827 when the allied fleets destroyed the combined Turkish and Egyptian fleets in two hours. This meant a change in the balance of power in the Mediterranean which Canning's policy had been designed to avoid but Canning was already dead. He had died, after a sudden illness, on 8 August less than four months after he had left the Foreign Office to become Prime Minister.

Part Two: Analysis

3 Lord Palmerston as Foreign Secretary

When Canning became Prime Minister in April 1827 he appointed Lord Dudley as Foreign Secretary, an office which Dudley retained during the brief administration of Lord Goderich and for a short time after the Duke of Wellington formed his government in January 1828. But it was accepted that Dudley had been placed at the Foreign Office by Canning to continue his own policy and Dudley never developed an independent line. In June 1828 Lord Aberdeen replaced him as Foreign Secretary.

The outstanding question was still the Greek war of independence. Wellington was seriously alarmed at the probable effect on the balance of power in the eastern Mediterranean of a Turkish collapse. Aberdeen, a classical scholar of some note who had organised some of the earliest archaeological excavations in Athens in 1803, was more sympathetic to the Greeks but he too was anxious to keep an independent Greece, which was likely to be under Russian influence, within narrow limits (36). War had broken out between Russia and Turkey in April 1828, and in September 1829 the Russians secured the Treaty of Adrianople. It gave them a virtual protectorate over Moldavia and Wallachia, lying in a vital strategic position at the mouth of the Danube. Russia's actual territorial gains were small but she insisted on the reaffirmation of earlier treaties which gave her ill-defined rights of intervention to protect various groups within the Ottoman empire. In fact the Tsar's government, after careful consideration, had come to the conclusion that the preservation, rather than the break up, of the ramshackle Ottoman empire would serve Russian interests best but this was not known to the outside world which was highly suspicious of Russian ambitions (5) [doc. 21]. After the Turkish defeat the original proposals for an autonomous but not independent Greece, confined to the Morea and a few islands, seemed quite inadequate. A settlement was finally reached in February 1830 by which the three powers, Russia, Britain and France, guaranteed an independent Greece south of a line drawn between the gulfs of Volvo and Arta; northern Greece and the island of Crete, one of the centres of the rebellion, remained in Turkish hands [doc. 23].

Domestic affairs rather than foreign policy occupied the minds of most Englishmen (including politicians) in the late 1820s and early 1830s. This was the period of the 'three Cs': Corn Laws, currency reform and Catholic Emancipation. To these there was now added parliamentary reform, first considered in the 1780s but held back for a generation by the distractions and alarms of the revolutionary wars and their aftermath. In July 1830 a new revolution broke out in France. The King, Charles X, and his ultra-conservative supporters were overthrown and Charles replaced by his Orleanist cousin, Louis-Philippe, who promised to govern as a constitutional king. This revolution coincided with a general election in Britain. The Prime Minister, Wellington, expected that events in France would actually help his government by reviving the fears of the property-owning electorate but party discipline of the modern kind did not exist in 1830 and it was not clear even when Parliament reassembled in November whether or not Wellington still commanded a majority. He misread the situation and, praising the perfection of the British constitution, committed himself to a policy of no change. The government lost a crucial vote and Wellington was succeeded as Prime Minister by Lord Grey, one of the few Whigs who had advocated parliamentary reform all along and had never rallied to Pitt's side. Until the passage of the Great Reform Act in 1832 neither Parliament nor the country had much time to spare for foreign problems.

The domestic events of the late 1820s had broken up the wide coalition of interests which had held together for so long under Lord Liverpool. Wellington and the ultra-Tories, together with some men who were later to emerge as moderates, such as Sir Robert Peel, formed one party, eventually to be called the Conservatives. Canning's supporters drifted towards the Whigs. One such Canningite was Henry John Temple, Third Viscount Palmerston.

Palmerston was born in London in October 1784. Although his title was an Irish one and the family had Irish estates, in which he took a close and generally enlightened interest, he did not have an Irish background as Castlereagh did. The main family estates were centred on Broadlands in Hampshire and Palmerston was educated at Harrow and the universities of Edinburgh and Cambridge. The decision to send the young Harry Temple to Edinburgh university was not an unusual one about 1800. It had a far better academic reputation than Oxford or Cambridge and he was permanently influenced by his professor, Dugald Stewart, a disciple of Adam Smith and an economist of note (78).

Palmerston at first experienced some difficulty in securing a parliamentary seat. He stood unsuccessfully for the Cambridge University seat after the death of Pitt but, like Canning, he was eventually fixed up with a rotten borough in the Isle of Wight. It was the beginning of an extremely long parliamentary career. He had been offered a government post as Junior Lord of the Admiralty even before he secured his seat and there were only two administrations between his entry into Parliament in 1807 and his death in 1865 in which he did not hold office **(103)**. Nevertheless he remained in junior office for an abnormally long time. In 1809 he refused a chance to become Chancellor of the Exchequer and instead became Secretary at War, without a seat in the Cabinet; he remained at the War Office until 1830 although he was brought into the Cabinet by Canning in 1827. During these years he impressed men as hard-working and competent but, astonishingly in view of his later reputation, as diffident and rather lacking in drive **(78)**. Possibly Palmerston's heart was not entirely in his parliamentary career. His father had been a dilettante, more interested in literature and society than in politics, who, although he was an M.P. for forty years, never aspired to more than very junior office. The younger Palmerston might have had a very similar career if he had not, when a member of Canning's Cabinet, for the first time had access to Cabinet papers, including the foreign despatches, and found his interest caught.

When Grey became Prime Minister in 1830 he offered Palmerston the Foreign Office. Despite his long years at the War Office, Palmerston had little experience of foreign affairs and it was at one time suggested that Grey himself really controlled policy during Palmerston's early years at the Foreign Office. The detailed researches of Professor Webster disproved that suggestion **(101)** but Grey, like most Prime Ministers, did keep in close touch with foreign affairs. Palmerston had certain advantages, including a fluent command of French, then the langague of diplomacy. As a child he had travelled with his family in France and Italy. Indeed as a child of seven he had been in Paris at the time of the storming of the Tuileries on 10 August 1792 and his family had themselves had a narrow escape from the revolutionaries. His maiden speech in the Commons had been on the Copenhagen expedition when he made an effective speech in defence of the government's right to regard Britain's vital interests as their first consideration. His next major speech on foreign affairs did not come until 1 June 1829 when he vigorously attacked the government's niggardliness towards the Greek's national aspirations, intending to set up a Greece 'which should contain neither Athens, nor Thebes, nor Marathon, nor Salamis, nor Plataea, nor Thermopylae, nor Missolonghi'. With the advantage of hindsight the later Palmerston can be seen emerging in these speeches.

In the 1830s Palmerston had to face the consequences of a number of challenges to the Vienna Settlement. When he took office the most pressing problem was Belgium and it remained with him for the rest of the decade. The decision to unite Belgium with Holland under the House of Orange had not seemed an unreasonable one in 1815. Apart from the question of providing a stronger barrier to French aggression, the economy of Belgium, which was already comparatively industrialised, seemed to form a natural complement to the predominantly trading economy of the Dutch, with their overseas empire and large carrying trade. The importance of the linguistic and religious differences between the two countries can be exaggerated: there were many Catholics in Holland and the linguistic divide between French and Flemish ran through Belgium, not along the Dutch–Belgian border. It was the maladroit policy of the Dutch king, William I, rather than any irreconcilable differences, which alienated his Belgian subjects (**21**). Inspired by the success of the July revolution in France, the Belgians rose in August 1830 and succeeded in expelling the Dutch. The Dutch King prepared to bring an army against them while the new monarchy of Louis-Philippe in France showed its support for Belgium.

The situation was perilous. If the French intervened on the Belgian side, the Austrians, Prussians and Russians would probably intervene on the Dutch side. A conference was convened in London on 4 November 1830, chaired by the British Foreign Secretary, Lord Aberdeen, and attended by the ambassadors of the great powers and of Holland, with (despite Dutch protests) a Belgian observer. When Palmerston succeeded Aberdeen on 22 November he had already made up his mind about his basic position. He wrote a few days later: 'his Majesty's Government consider the absolute and entire separation of Belgium from Holland to be no longer a matter for discussion, but to have become, by the course of events, an established, and as far as can at present be foreseen, an irreversible fact' (**101**). Many questions, however, remained to be settled; the form of government of the new state, its frontiers and the fate of the Duchy of Luxemburg, which had also been placed under the House of Orange in 1815 but which the Belgians now claimed.

An armistice was arranged by the powers in January 1831 while discussions continued, but in August 1831 an exasperated William I invaded Belgium and won considerable success. A French army came to the support of the Belgians and the Dutch were compelled to withdraw. A British fleet took up a watchful position off the Belgian coast. The situation was once again very tense. A tentative settlement had already been arrived at in January 1831 [**doc. 25**] which would have given

Belgium the frontiers of the old Austrian Netherlands but allowed William to retain the Duchy of Luxemburg. In the spring of 1831 the Belgians had been persuaded to relinquish any hope of electing the Duke of Nemours, a younger son of Louis-Philippe, as their king – an arrangement naturally favoured by the French – and instead to offer the throne to Leopold of Saxe-Coburg. Leopold was a compromise candidate. He was the bereaved husband of George IV's only daughter, Charlotte, and was believed to be an Anglophile, but he was about to marry Louis-Philippe's daughter, Louise. After August 1831 Palmerston devoted his energies to salvaging these arrangements. He was ultimately successful but success took a long time. The main obstacle was the obstinacy of William I **(21, 101)**.

Military measures were again resorted to in the course of 1832. Palmerston now tried a technique he was to employ many times throughout his long career, that of curtailing the freedom of action of potential adversaries by allying with them. If William I must be coerced it should be by joint Anglo-French action. In December 1832 a French force expelled the Dutch from Antwerp while a combined British and French fleet blockaded the Dutch coast and the mouth of the Scheldt. A new armistice was concluded in 1833 but the final settlement was delayed until 1839 when, by the Treaty of London of 19 May, most of the terms of the original *Bases de Séparation* of 1831 [doc. 25] were at last enforced. A most important clause was the guarantee of Belgian neutrality given by all the great powers. It was not unprecedented. The neutrality of Switzerland had been guaranteed at Vienna [doc. 15]. But it was rightly regarded as an important step in the search for a lasting peace in Europe since it removed one very sensitive area from conflict. It was respected until the German invasion in 1914. The Belgian question is generally regarded as an example of Palmerstonian policy as its best, when he showed not only firmness and decisiveness but also the tact and patience which he so often lacked. He was, of course, helped by the fact that the new government of Louis-Philippe, unsure how far it was accepted by the eastern powers, was anxious to be on good terms with England **(29)**.

Where conditions were less favourable, there was comparatively little that Palmerston could do. In November 1830 the Poles rose against the Tsar's rule. Nicholas not only crushed them with severity but extinguished even the fiction of Polish independence by incorporating the country into Russia. Public opinion in Britain, and still more in France, was on the side of the Poles and radical pressure groups in Parliament urged Palmerston to take action. He was well aware that he could do no such thing. Only a successful land war could have made the Russians change their policy and there was no question of Britain being able to launch such a war.

He was scarcely more successful in the representations he made in Italy. In February 1831 there were insurrections in the Papal States and in Parma and Modena. The July Monarchy made some gestures of support towards the insurgents. In Britain anti-Papal feeling still ran high and once again radical groups urged Palmerston to take action. Palmerston, however, attempted no more than using his influence to prevent a Franco-Austrian clash, for the Austrians had set their faces against any changes in Italy. He urged the Pope and other rulers to consider moderate concessions but he was powerless when they rejected his advice. It is scarcely surprising that in his first few years at the Foreign Office, in contrast to his later reputation, Palmerston was regarded as a weak and ineffectual Foreign Secretary who attracted satirical comments from both Tories and Radicals. The Tories saw him as a deserter who had joined the Whigs solely to retain office, while he further antagonised the radicals by his lukewarm attitude to parliamentary reform. He made one speech during this period [**doc. 26**], which was later to be much quoted as evidence of the liberal principles in which he referred to constitutional states as Britain's 'natural allies' but even this was in the context of explaining that he could do nothing to help German dissidents against Metternich's anti-revolutionary policies, (78).

Palmerston's public reputation was improved by his handling of the still difficult problems of the Iberian Peninsula, but here too his early interventions did not appear very successful. In Portugal the British support for Maria had collapsed after the death of Canning, and in June 1828 Miguel had been proclaimed King and Maria had returned to Brazil. Miguel's rule, although apparently firmly entrenched, was arbitrary and a number of British and French traders complained of mistreatment. In 1831 the French, with British approval, sent a fleet to Lisbon. This coincided with the entry of the French army into Belgium and allowed Wellington himself to say in the Lords that, whereas in Napoleon's time Britain had fought the Peninsular War and the battle of Waterloo to keep France out of Portugal and the Low Countries, Palmerston was now conniving at France's presence in both (78).

British opinion was better pleased when Palmerston extended his diplomatic support to Pedro, who decided to come to his daughter's assistance in Portugal. His only base was at first the island of Terceira in the Azores but he was reinforced by British and French volunteers.

The British volunteers, of whom the most famous was the sailor (later Admiral) Charles Napier, had to find a way round the Foreign Enlistment Act which forbade British subjects to enlist in foreign armies, but the government was not disposed to make difficulties. Pedro landed in Portugal in July 1832 but he found more support for Miguel than he had expected and at first he could not break out of his base at Oporto. The following July Napier defeated Miguel's fleet off Cape St Vincent and Pedro captured Lisbon, but Miguel was not finally defeated until 1834.

Spain too was rent by conflict between absolutists and 'Liberals' in the 1830s. King Ferdinand VII died in September 1833. The succession was disputed between the supporters of Isabella, Ferdinand's young daughter, and her mother Christina, who had been proclaimed Regent during her daughter's minority, and the supporters of Ferdinand's brother, Carlos, who contended that Ferdinand had had no right to set aside the Salic Law which forbade the accession of a woman to the Spanish throne. Carlos had the support of the absolutists; consequently, the Liberals rallied to Isabella's side. At first Christina's regency seemed fairly firmly established but it was known that the three eastern powers favoured Carlos's cause. The Emperor of Austria, the King of Prussia and the Tsar of Russia met in the autumn of 1833 to discuss a number of questions of mutual interest. Nicholas and Francis signed an agreement at Münchengratz in September 1833 to which Frederick William became a party (101). They pledged themselves to the defence of absolutism and one of the minor effects of the agreement was the sending of financial assistance to Don Carlos.

Palmerston determined on a counterstroke, which he later described as 'a capital hit and all my own doing'. This was the famous Quadruple Alliance signed in April 1834 between Britain, France, Queen Christina of Spain and Queen Maria of Portugal [doc. 27]. Christina and Maria undertook to exclude Carlos and Miguel from their respective countries, the British undertook to supply a naval force, and the French promised to prevent aid reaching Carlos through France — Palmerston effectively discouraged any military intervention by Louis Philippe.

In May Carlos and Miguel both surrendered to the Admiral commanding the British force (78). So far as Portugal was concerned that was virtually the end of the matter. Miguel retired to Rome to live as a private citizen. In 1836 Maria was married to another Saxe-Coburg, Ferdinand, the nephew of Leopold of the Belgians and, at least in theory, a strictly constitutional government was established, in which Queen Victoria was to take a great personal interest. Spain was not so easily settled. Carlos reduced Palmerston's successful stroke to a farce when, after a few weeks exile in England, he slipped away to rejoin his forces in northern Spain where the Basque separatists, who disliked the Liberals' centralising policy, supported him. It took another six years to end the endemic war. Neither Britain nor France could resist fishing in the murky waters. Palmerston secured the suspension of the Foreign Enlistment Act to allow British volunteers to fight on Christina's side. He was dragged further than he meant to go, even finding himself supporting the radicals as the only alternative to the so-called moderates (*Moderados*) who had become identified with the French interest.

Palmerston's success in settling the affairs of the Iberian Peninsula was in reality limited but he remained fairly satisfied with it; he believed that he had prevented any more active French intervention. The idea of the alliance of 'four constitutional states' proved popular in Britain. Palmerston began to see the possibilities of a new kind of balance in Europe, liberal states against absolute monarchies. He said, 'The treaty establishes among the constitutional states of the West, a Quadruple Alliance which will serve as a counterpoise against the Holy Alliance of the East,' but that was rhetoric. The Quadruple Alliance made up of two unstable states and two suspicious rivals, was a fragile instrument compared with the Münchengratz agreement (**13, 78, 101**).

The Münchengratz discussions had been focused as much on the Eastern Question as on the progress of liberalism in western Europe. The three powers agreed to uphold the integrity of Turkey for as long as possible but to concert their policies if, in spite of their efforts, the Ottoman empire collapsed. One problem, Greece, seemed for the time being to be solved. By an agreement signed in London in 1832 between Britain, France and Russia [**doc. 24**], a monarchy had been set up there under Otto, the seventeen-year-old son of the King of Bavaria. Otto did not prove to be a good choice: Palmerston later referred to his selection as 'the worst day's work I ever did'. Otto refused to grant the Greeks a constitution but this did not stop rival parties forming who looked either to Britain or to France for sympathy, much as they did in Spain. Another complication was the Greeks' firm intention not to accept the restricted boundaries assigned to them in 1830 but to regain all the lands, including Crete, which they regarded as their ancient territories.

The most immediate threat to the Ottoman empire came, however, from Egypt. The ruler of Egypt since 1805 had been Mehemet Ali, an Albanian soldier who had arrived in Egypt during the Napoleonic wars. Egypt was still part of the Turkish empire and Mehemet Ali was merely the Pasha or Governor, removable at the Sultan's pleasure, but he was an extremely strong ruler and a great admirer of Napoleon Bonaparte. French influence remained strong in Egypt. Mehemet Ali employed French advisers to reorganise his army and introduce more modern methods of agriculture. The Egyptian educational and legal systems were reorganised on French models. Mehemet Ali's troops conquered a large part of the Sudan. When the Sultan, Mahmud II, asked for the help of Mehemet Ali's adopted son, Ibrahim, to subdue the Greeks (see chapter 2), he promised him Crete and Syria as a reward. Ibrahim would almost certainly have succeeded in his task but for the intervention of the Great Powers and he was moved to protest when the Sultan cut his reward down to Crete. In 1831 he invaded Syria and, despite the resistance of Acre, within twelve months he had conquered Syria and Palestine. In December 1832 he defeated the main Turkish army at Konieh and began to advance towards the Bosphorus. In his extremity the Sultan appealed to Britain for aid. Palmerston himself would have been willing to give it but he could not persuade the Cabinet. Some years later he wrote to Frederick Lamb, the British Ambassador at Vienna:

> There is nothing that has happened since I have been in this office which I regret so much as that tremendous blunder of the English government. But it was not my fault . . . Grey, who was with me on the point, was weak and gave way, and so nothing was done in a crisis of the utmost importance to all Europe, when we might with the greatest of ease have accomplished a good result (**78, 92**).

The Sultan then turned to Russia as, one of his officials said, 'a drowning man clings to a serpent'. A Russian squadron entered the Bosphorus in February 1833. Ibrahim retreated. On 8 July the Turks concluded the Treaty of Unkiar Skelessi [**doc. 28**]. Essentially it was a defensive alliance but the most important article was a secret one by which the Sultan agreed to close the Dardanelles to all foreign warships, if the Russians requested it. The previous month Mehemet Ali had proposed an anti-Russian alliance to Palmerston. This, Palmerston was not prepared to accept: Mehemet Ali did not represent a sovereign power, Egypt being still within the Turkish empire, but in any case such a policy would have carried unacceptable risks. Although Britain was uneasy about Russian forward moves in Central Asia, which might one day present a threat to British India, Palmerston had no wish to launch a crusade against Russia, although he was urged to do so by radicals, who could not forgive Russian brutalities in Poland (**78**). Consequently, France remained the chief patron of Mehemet Ali.

The uneasy *status quo* was maintained in the Near East until 1839.

In April 1839 the Turks invaded Syria, still under Ibrahim's rule. It was the revenge the Turks had been waiting for since 1833. Mahmoud had not dared to attack until his army was reorganised but he was now a dying man and determined to delay no longer. Once again Ibrahim had little difficulty in defeating the Turks and the way to Constantinople seemed to be open. On 1 July 1839 Mahmoud died and was succeeded by Abdul Mejid, a boy of sixteen. All the great powers were seriously alarmed. The dissolution of the Ottoman empire seemed to be at hand and they quickly manoeuvred for diplomatic positions (92).

France still favoured the granting of considerable concessions to Mehemet Ali but, in the spring of 1839, Britain and Russia had begun to concert their policy. To some extent Palmerston employed the same tactic towards Russia over the Eastern Question as he had done towards France in western Europe, that is allying with her in order to influence her policy (101), but he also had deep suspicions of the French interest in Egypt, especially after the French conquest of Algiers in the 1830s. An Anglo-French fleet did indeed proceed to the Dardanelles with a watching brief, but Palmerston also proposed an international conference similar to the one on Belgium. He would have preferred it to have met in London but agreed readily enough that it should meet in Vienna (102). He hoped at first that Mehemet Ali would be deprived of his control of Syria and it is hard to resist the impression that there was a note of personal antagonism in Palmerston's suspicions of Mehemet Ali. He wrote to Lord Granville, the British Ambassador in Paris, in June 1839, 'I hate Mehemet Ali, whom I consider as nothing better than an ignorant barbarian who by cunning and mother wit has been successful in rebellion . . . I look upon his boasted civilization of Egypt as an arrantist humbug, and I believe that he is as great a tyrant and oppressor as ever made a people wretched' (78).

Ibrahim's victories and the death of Mahmoud, however, made immediate strong action against Mehemet Ali impracticable. Mehemet Ali, realising the dangers of the enmity of the great powers, exercised restraint and ordered Ibrahim to limit his pursuit of the Turks. From the beginning there had been a divergence of attitude between France and the other powers and, when Thiers became the French Prime Minister in March 1840, he came out firmly in support of the Egyptians. Previously Palmerston had made several attempts to concert his policy with the French [doc. 29] but now he did not hesitate to join the other three powers and Turkey in an agreement to which France was not a party, the Convention of July 1840 [doc. 30]. By this the powers agreed to offer Mehemet Ali Egypt 'for his house' (that is, it was to become hereditary in his family) and part of Syria 'for his lifetime'. If Mehemet Ali did not accept these offers promptly they would be withdrawn and the powers made it clear that they were prepared to back their words with armed force.

In London the traditionally Francophile Whigs were indignant at this treatment of their 'ally' and Palmerston became extremely unpopular with an important section of his own party, some of whom did not hesitate to discuss his delinquencies with their French friends, including Thiers himself [doc. 32]. In fact as Palmerston was aware, there was very little that the French could do about the situation. When Mehemet Ali remained obstinate, Acre was bombarded, and eventually he submitted to the terms dictated by the four powers. The agreement of July 1840 was partially superseded the following July by the Straits Convention, to which France was a party together with the other powers, which abrogated the secret clauses of the Treaty of Unkiar Skelessi — which had already been allowed to lapse — by reaffirming the ancient convention that the Dardanelles should be closed to all foreign warships while Turkey was at peace.

Palmerston had been largely successful in the resolution of the Eastern crisis of 1840 in conjunction with the three eastern powers but he had not only separated England from France, he had displayed an insouciance about the whole affair which brought down on his head the very opposite charges to those of timidity, with which he had been assailed when he first came into office. Charles Greville, the diarist, wrote of him at this time,

Everything may possibly turn out according to his expectations. He is a man blessed with extraordinary good fortune, and his motto seems to be that of Danton, *De l'audace* . . . But there is a flippancy in his tone, an undoubting self-sufficiency, and a levity in discussing interests of such tremendous magnitude, which satisfies me that he is a very dangerous man to be entrusted with the uncontrolled management of our foreign affairs (42, 78).

Palmerston's handling of the Chinese question also attracted criticism, although from a much smaller section of opinion. Since the eighteenth century British merchants had been trying to build up trade with China; there was an apparently insatiable demand for Chinese luxury goods, tea, silks and porcelain, in the West but the Manchu government in China was cool towards western traders. There were two main problems. The Manchus consistently refused to open what the West regarded as normal diplomatic relations between states which the Chinese persisted in regarding as unimportant 'barbarians' beyond the seas. Secondly, there were very few European goods which the Chinese wanted in return and in the mercantilist period of the eighteenth century the British government had not been happy to see Chinese goods paid for in bullion. There was, however, a demand for opium in China and the British East India Company had found that it could make a good profit by growing opium in India and exporting it to China in return for Chinese merchandise. Opium smoking was to some extent tolerated in China and for a time the Chinese authorities hesitated whether to ban these new opium imports or simply to regulate them. In the late 1830s the party which wished to ban them won and a certain Commissioner Lin was despatched to Canton to enforce this. Lin, however, found it impossible to take effective action against British ships off the coast. Instead he subjected the British merchant community in Canton, including the British consul, Charles Elliot, to a form of house arrest. The British appealed to their authorities in India, who sent a squadron of frigates which had no difficulty in defeating the junks which the Chinese sent against them. The Opium War had begun before London was really aware of the fact (13, 78).

The morality of the opium trade played a smaller part in the ensuing debate than a later generation might expect. The young William Gladstone's strong denunciation of British actions[doc. 33] was exceptional. Palmerston did not question the Chinese government's right to ban the trade, although he was cynical enough to think that economics, rather than morality, had occasioned the Chinese stand. 'There is an opium-growing interest in China as there is a corn-growing interest in England,' he said. Britain had no right to protect opium smugglers, but that was not the question. The peaceable British trading community at Canton, not all of whom were implicated in the opium trade, had been molested and put in fear of their lives. Here there was, although it was not recognised at the time, a real clash between eastern and western concepts of law. The Chinese believed that the community to which a malefactor belonged could properly be held responsible for his actions. Such an idea of collective responsibility was alien to the British. The innocent should not be punished with the guilty and the British merchants had at least been through an alarming experience. Moreover, the fact that the action had been extended to Elliot offended all western ideas of diplomatic immunity and raised the old question of proper diplomatic recognition by the Chinese.

The war was still in progress when the Whig administration fell from office. Peel's Conservative government made no significant change in policy. The end came with the treaty of Nanking in 1842 when China opened certain ports, the 'treaty ports', to British trade at agreed rates of duty and the British annexed the island of Hong Kong to be a base under British control.

The end of the Whig government also found British relations with the United States in considerable disarray. Three matters had contributed to this: slavery, the continued existence of the British colony of Canada on North American soil and the problem of Texas, which derived ultimately from the break up of the Spanish empire in America (4, 16, 19).

The United States, like Britain, had declared the Slave Trade, the transportation of Negroes from Africa, illegal in 1807. It had occasionally been suggested that the Slave Trade should be equated with piracy, which would have given a warship of any nation the right to take action against a slaver just as she could take action against a pirate, but national susceptibilities had always proved too strong for this solution to be adopted. Consequently, in the absence of any specific treaty on the subject, a warship could only intercept a slaver flying her own national colours. She had no jurisdiction over other ships, no matter how blatant the offence. Britain was the only nation which kept a squadron on the West African coast with any degree of consistency to suppress the trade. After the denunciation of the trade at the Congress of Vienna, Britain had signed treaties, the so-called Right of Search treaties, with a number of nations, empowering British warships to stop and search suspected slavers flying that country's flag. Many people in Britain felt passionately about the trade and Palmerston seems to have genuinely and wholeheartedly shared their detestation [doc. 34]. He devoted much time and energy to the subject and he negotiated many treaties, including two with France in 1831 and 1833, to suppress the Trade. In 1838 he set out to involve all the great powers of Europe in one such treaty, the Quintuple Treaty. The Eastern crisis, however, intervened and, to mark their displeasure at Palmerston's conduct, the French government refused to ratify it.

Britain and the United States had never signed a right of search treaty. The stumbling block on the American side was partly the use of the right of search and impressment which Britain had made during the Napoleonic wars. (Impressment was the right to remove British sailors from foreign ships in time of war to 'press' them into the Royal Navy.) Palmerston readily conceded that in the absence of a treaty British warships could not search an American ship in peacetime but he was angered by the fact that slavers of other nationalities, with whom Britain did have treaties, hoisted the Stars and Stripes to escape the British cruisers. He therefore argued for a 'right of visit' to a suspected ship to make sure that she was entitled to the colours she was flying. They should not, he said, be allowed to escape simply because they hoisted 'a piece of bunting'. The Americans refused to countenance the idea of a right of visit and American propaganda angrily complained that Palmerston had referred to the American flag as a 'piece of bunting' (4).

Another question relating to slavery also inflamed Anglo-American relations. In 1833 slavery itself had been abolished in the British empire. Henceforth a man could not be a slave on British soil. It sometimes happened that an American ship carrying slaves, quite legally by American law, between American ports was driven by bad weather into a British West Indian port. In several instances the British took the view that any slaves on board immediately became free men. This angered the Americans, partly because they feared it would encourage slaves on board ship to mutiny and put into a British port. Their anger also reflected a general suspicion that the British had ruined the economy of the British West Indies by the emancipation of the slaves and now wished to ruin their American competitors by forcing the same course on them. Even darker suspicions existed that the British thought that in any future war between the two countries, the slaves would be America's Trojan horse. 'We need send few troops if we sent a million rifles to Kentucky,' one grim theorist is supposed to have suggested.

The most likely cause of a war seemed to be the continued existence of Canada, or British North America to give it its correct name at this period. Many boundary questions remained unsettled but, more than that, many Americans believed that the continued existence of any British colony on North American soil was intolerable and, furthermore, that the Canadians really wished to be 'liberated'. Two small-scale rebellions in Upper and Lower Canada (the modern Ontario and Quebec) in 1837–38 gave colour to this belief and some gun-running took place across the frontier. In the course of this a small American steamer, the *Caroline*, was sunk in the Niagara River (although it did not plunge blazing over Niagara Falls as contemporary legend said), and an American citizen called Durfee was killed in the affray. In November 1840 a Canadian, Alexander McLeod, was arrested while doing business on the American side of the border and charged with Durfee's murder. It is unlikely that McLeod, had been anywhere near the scene at the time of Durfee's death but in any case the British government immediately informed the American government that Durfee's death was properly a matter between the two countries and an individual could not be held responsible. Palmerston told the British Minister in Washington, Henry Fox, to leave immediately if McLeod were executed. The Americans took the extraordinary step of saying they would prevent Fox from leaving. The Federal Government was in a very awkward situation because McLeod had been arrested on the authority of the State of New York and any attempt to override their jurisdiction would have raised the most difficult questions of States' rights. The matter was still unresolved when Palmerston left office.

Palmerston also became involved with the problem of Texas. In 1836 Texas broke away from Mexico and formed an independent republic. The Texans, many of whom were immigrants from the States, asked to join the American Union, but for domestic reasons the northern States at first opposed this and in 1837 the Texans sent agents to all the leading commercial powers of Europe to secure commercial treaties and loans. The British saw advantages in Texan independence. An independent Texas might balance the power of the United States and prevent the latter from gaining preponderance in the Caribbean. If Texas became an important cotton producer outside the American tariff system, she might free Britain from her dangerous dependence on United States' cotton. Finally, British abolitionists hoped that Texas might be persuaded to abolish slavery (which was not yet highly developed there) in return for political or commercial concessions. Palmerston therefore readily signed three treaties with the Texan representative, General Hamilton, in November 1840. The first was a commercial treaty; the second offered British mediation between Texas and Mexico, who still claimed jurisdiction in Texas; the third provided for a mutual right of search to suppress the Slave Trade.

The years 1830–41 have generally been regarded by historians as the most consistently successful of Palmerston's long career, when he had a nice appreciation of the forces in Europe and when he brought all his major policies and stratagems to a successful conclusion. Contemporaries took a rather different view. The complexities of the long negotiations over questions such as Belgium were not understood **(101)**. In 1841 the political world – the men whose views counted – saw him as the man who had estranged France and embroiled Britain in wearisome disputes with the United States. Palmerston himself was furious at losing office just when he felt that all his policies were going well and most of his objectives in sight but many others heaved sighs of relief when he gave place to the Earl of Aberdeen.

4 Palmerston and Aberdeen: Two Rival Schools?

The Whigs finally relinquished office in September 1841. They were succeeded by the conservative government of Sir Robert Peel. Peel's administration was the strongest to emerge between the Reform Acts of 1832 and 1867. It was not an uneasy coalition of disparate elements as all the Whig governments were, or as Lord Aberdeen's coalition was to be in 1852. It had a clear majority in the Commons and a coherent programme, based ultimately on the principles of the Tamworth Manifesto: of conserving what was good and remedying what was amiss. Peel hoped for an orderly conduct of foreign affairs to supplement and strengthen a policy of moderate reform at home. His first choice for Foreign Secretary had been the Duke of Wellington, who had held that office during the short conservative administration of 1834–35. Wellington, however, had had a stroke in 1840 and, although much recovered, still did not feel well enough to take on the Foreign Office. In his place Peel appointed George Gordon, Fourth Earl of Aberdeen.

It was an unexceptional choice. Aberdeen was not well known to the public but he too was a disciple of William Pitt, who had already been Foreign Secretary in 1828–30. His connection with Pitt was a close one. Aberdeen's father, Lord Haddo, had died when his son was seven. Because of complicated family feuds his grandfather, the Third Earl, had wanted nothing to do with his grandson and had been reluctant even to pay for his education at Harrow and Cambridge. At the age of fourteen the future Fourth Earl used his right under Scots law to name his own guardians. He chose Henry Dundas (who readily agreed because he hoped to control the Gordon electoral interest in Scotland) and Dundas's friend, William Pitt. Henceforth the boy was encouraged to look on Pitt's home at Wimbledon as his own and Pitt inspired in him a determination to enter public life. The branch of the Gordon family to which Aberdeen belonged had not been prominent in politics in the eighteenth century. Apart from the character of the Third Earl, their convictions as Jacobites and non-jurors had closed many doors to them. Perhaps the Fourth Earl (he succeeded to the title in 1801) would have been a happier man if he had followed his own bent as a reforming landlord and pioneering archaeologist but from an early age his career turned in the direction of diplomacy. During the Peace of Amiens he travelled on the continent and met Napoleon. He then joined the British Ambassador to Constantinople and travelled extensively in Greece and the Levant, an adventurous undertaking in the early 1800s. In 1805 he married Lady Catherine Hamilton, the daughter of the powerful Marquess of Abercorn. His political future looked bright when his hopes were shattered by Pitt's death in 1806. Like Palmerston, Aberdeen thought of entering the Commons by standing for the Cambridge University seat left vacant by Pitt's death but there were constitutional difficulties arising from his Scottish peerage and instead he became one of the representative peers of Scotland in the House of Lords. In 1807 Canning offered him the embassy to Sicily and in 1809 he was offered the embassy to Russia. He declined both appointments. He was absorbed in his attempts to improve the condition of his Scottish estates, left in a decaying state by his grandfather, and in his young family. Tragedy, however, was soon to strike. His adored wife died of tuberculosis in 1812 and the three daughters of the marriage were to succumb to the same disease in the 1820s. Aberdeen not infrequently withdrew from public life in a vain attempt to save their lives by removing them to warmer climates abroad (36).

After his wife's death, his political associates again hoped that Aberdeen might be persuaded to take public office. He refused the mission to the United States but in 1813 he accepted the embassy to Austria (see chapter 2). The mission was to have a profound effect on him. He set off with some feeling of excitement at seeing the war at first hand. Within a few weeks he was sickened and the conviction that war was a barbarous business which almost nothing could justify, never left him [doc. 35].

The mission also gave him the opportunity to meet the leading figures of Europe and he retained a genuine, although by no means uncritical, feeling of friendship for Metternich. Although he did not have any particular confidence in Congresses — as Foreign Secretary he even doubted the value of the kind of ambassadorial conferences favoured by Palmerston — his experiences gave him a European outlook on diplomacy which contrasted with the more insular and nationalistic views of Canning and Palmerston. This was a source of both strength and weakness too: it enabled him to approach conflicts in an almost judicial spirit and to look instinctively for a compromise solution, but it seemed to blind him to the element of bluff which is inseparable from international diplomacy. Palmerston once said that any nation would give up three questions out of four, rather than fight for them, but that it would be fatal to let one's opponent know this in advance

(21). Aberdeen rarely gave the impression that he would fight, and Palmerston, who believed that if only he had remained in office all the outstanding issues would have been resolved to Britain's advantage, commented in despair that British foreign policy had 'got on a sliding scale' **(13).**

The two most difficult problems when Aberdeen took up the reins at the Foreign Office were relations with America and relations with France. The simultaneous hostility of both presented real dangers for Britain. The thoughts of British statesmen went to the coalition of 1778. The Duke of Wellington gloomily prophesied that a war with the United States 'will not be with that power alone'. The combined maritime strength of France and the United States was the only one which could have seriously challenged British naval supremacy at this time. Aberdeen saw only three possible courses of action. He might have ridden out the storm, trusting in Britain's own strength and the reluctance of other powers to challenge it. This had been Palmerston's policy in the 1830s and it had its attractions for Wellington and, to some extent, for Peel in the 1840s. It did not appeal to Aberdeen. Secondly, he might have drawn closer to the eastern powers, Austria, Russia and Prussia, to provide a counterweight. He did pursue this policy to a limited extent but he doubted the material power of both Austria and Prussia (he told his brother, Sir Robert Gordon, who became British ambassador in Vienna, 'I look on Austria very much in the same light as Turkey, and as almost null in the scale of nations'), and he found the Tsar, Nicholas I, upredictable. This left only the third option, reconciliation and a return to good relations with both France and the United States. This was the most congenial to Aberdeen's own temperament and the opportunity seemed to be there. The moderate Guizot had replaced the belligerent Thiers as Prime Minister of France and the equally moderate John Tyler and Daniel Webster had become respectively President and Secretary of State of the United States, although unfortunately Tyler was soon to be at odds with his own Congress and to experience difficulty in controlling it.

Relations with the United States were to assume larger proportions in British foreign policy in the 1840s than at any other time between the war of 1812 and the American Civil War. There were four main issues, the final settlement of the Canadian boundary, the right of search, the McLeod case and the *Creole* case. The *Creole* was an American ship which had been taken by mutinous slaves and steered into the British port of Nassau. The Americans demanded the return at least of those men who had killed the ship's officers. The McLeod case was the most pressing. On 18 October 1841 Peel, Aberdeen and other ministers actually met to discuss the deployment of the British fleet in the event of war (16). McLeod stood his trial but was acquitted.

The possibility of a general settlement was canvassed in the American press and an informal approach made to the British government through the great banking firm of Baring Brothers, which conducted much American business. Aberdeen resolved to send out a member of the firm, Lord Ashburton, as a special envoy. Ashburton was a leading Conservative peer with excellent contacts, but he was also an elderly man, reluctant to face gruelling negotiations in Washington and even more convinced than Aberdeen himself that a general settlement was the thing to aim for and that the details of individual negotiations were comparatively unimportant.

Ashburton's instructions were drawn up in considerable haste, partly because Ashburton himself, who dreaded crossing the Atlantic, wanted to sail before the spring gales. Aberdeen seems to have done little research into the past history of the questions and to have consulted few colleagues. The most important question was the so-called North-East boundary, that is the boundary between Maine and New Brunswick which had been described in words in the Treaty of Versailles of 1783. No map had been annexed to the treaty and the intended line had become the subject of acrimonious dispute. The King of the Netherlands had been asked to mediate and had proposed a compromise line in 1831 but this had been rejected by the Americans. Aberdeen regarded the whole disputed territory as more or less valueless and originally empowered Ashburton to accept almost any sort of reasonable division [doc. 37]. When Wellington saw Aberdeen's instructions to Ashburton, he was horrified. Aberdeen, he contended, had missed the whole point. At all costs the Americans must be kept off the highlands just south of Quebec, and the road from Halifax to Quebec – the only route from Britain to the Canadas in winter when the St Lawrence was frozen – which crossed the disputed territory must be kept in British hands. In the end a compromise was worked out which left the road in British hands but divided the highlands. In the long run it proved satisfactory to both parties although the argument as to its justice went on for many years in Canada (16, 19).

The *Creole* case was also disposed of. The British maintained that, as they had no extradition treaty with the United States, the offenders could not legally be handed over. The Americans were indignant but the final result was the conclusion of a satisfactory extradition treaty between the two powers.

The right of search issues proved intractable. Ashburton begged Aberdeen to give up the right of impressment, which he believed was at the root of the trouble [doc. 38]. Aberdeen agreed that it was inconceivable in practice that the British navy would every again be able to impress British sailors from American ships but, perhaps remembering the storm over his supposed surrender of British maritime rights in 1813, he firmly declined to make any formal renunciation. There was in fact a difficult problem of constitutional law involved. Britain did not yet recognise what would today be called 'naturalisation'. Ashburton wrote to Webster,

America, receiving every year by thousands the emigrants of Europe, maintains the doctrine suitable to her condition of the right of transferring allegiance at will. The laws of Great Britain have maintained from all time the opposite doctrine. The duties of allegiance are held to be indefeasible.

The Americans conceded neither the right of search nor the right of visit; instead they agreed to maintain a squadron on the coast of West Africa to police American ships themselves. The squadron was never brought up to strength and vested interests in America were powerful enough to ensure that the American suppression of the Trade continued to be half-hearted.

The so-called 'joint cruising' arrangements, the extradition treaty and the north-east boundary settlement were incorporated in the Webster–Ashburton treaty and ratifications were finally exchanged in London on 13 October 1842. Palmerston attacked it as the 'Ashburton capitulation' but he got little support: most of the Whig leaders, Russell, Clarendon, Lansdowne, Spencer and Bedford, favoured it. *The Times* which was usually anti-American in tone, approved it. The diarist, Charles Greville, commented, 'He [Palmerston] ought to have felt the public pulse.... It is now evident that he will not carry the public nor even his own party with him' (13).

Public opinion approved the treaty but it did not achieve its fundamental purpose of creating relations of 'undisturbable Amity' with the United States. Daniel Webster continued to regard himself as a good friend of Britain and Aberdeen built up cordial relations with Edward Everett, the American minister in London but new storms soon appeared on the horizon.

American opinion was disturbed by the strong action Britain took against Brazil in the matter of the Slave Trade. In 1826 the Brazilians had granted the British the right of search over Brazilian slavers. In 1845, irritated by Britain's discriminatory duties against slave-grown sugar, they terminated the treaty. The British, in effect, ignored the Brazilian decision and claimed that as the Brazilians had once agreed that the Slave Trade was tantamount to piracy, any warship had the right to arrest a Brazilian slaver as a pirate. An Act was passed through Parliament in 1845 sanctioning this practice as it applied to Brazil: although certain Acts of the United States Congress had also equated slaving with piracy, Britain had no intention of trying to apply this doctrine to a major naval power. But the episode is an interesting example of Aberdeen being as willing as Palmerston to coerce a weak power when he thought the cause good enough (36).

Texas also continued to cause trouble. Mexico and Texas had gone to war and the Mexicans ordered two war-steamers from Britain, the *Guadeloupe* to be built at Liverpool and the *Montezuma* at London. The Texans protested but Aberdeen replied that British neutrality made it as proper for the Mexicans to buy arms in England as for the Texans to do so in the United States. He did, however, insist that it was illegal for private ships to be armed in British ports and the two vessels must take their arms as cargo. The Mexicans recruited two Royal Navy captains and a number of British sailors for the ships. An incident as serious as the famous *Alabama* case might have resulted but the two ships saw little action, although the *Guadeloupe* once engaged a Texan squadron under the British colours. Aberdeen's attitude led some people to suppose that, as a Conservative, he favoured the Mexican cause, but in fact he was much irritated by the Mexicans' arbitrary fiscal policy and their cavalier treatment of foreign, including British, nationals.

Palmerston's three treaties were ratified in June 1842 and Aberdeen tried to secure a joint Anglo-French mediation between Texas and Mexico. The British government was still very anxious that Texas should not join the United States and Aberdeen, urged on by the abolitionist lobby, spoke on the matter in Parliament in the summer of 1843; this speech caused much indignation in the United States. Mexico was uncooperative and British attempts to get a settlement were unavailing. Finally, President Tyler, anxious to leave office in a blaze of glory, secured the passage through Congress of resolutions in favour of the annexation of Texas in the spring of 1845 (36).

The northern states had abandoned their opposition to the admission of Texas because they wanted the support of the southern states in their own plans for Oregon. A convention of 1818 had recognised the 49th parallel as the boundary between the United States and British North America as far west as the Rocky Mountains. West of the Rockies the boundary was still undetermined. Ashburton had been empowered to negotiate on the question but it had not seemed urgent in 1842 and by mutual consent it had not been pursued. In 1842 Mexico still owned the territory south of the 42nd parallel, including San Francisco, while Russian claims to the land north of 54° 40' (the modern Alaska) had been recognised by both the United States and Britain. The two powers had a variety of historical claims to the land between 42° and 54° 40 and in 1818 had agreed to joint occupancy without prejudice to the claims of either. This was overtaken in the 1840s by the triumph of the 'Manifest Destiny' movement in the United States. *The Times* commented sourly: 'With a whole continent to range over they [the Americans] become as captious in asserting doubtful claims as a mediatised Prince of the German Empire.' In the 1840s thousands of Americans began to hit the Oregon trail, some going round Cape Horn or across the Isthmus of Panama. The area seriously in dispute between Britain and the United States was the triangle of land bounded by the Columbia River, the Pacific Ocean and the 49th parallel. The Columbia River was regarded as important because it was mistakenly believed to be potentially a great commercial highway to the Pacific. In terms of occupation Britain had rather the better claim because the Hudson's Bay Company had established settlements in the area.

Several opportunities to negotiate in a comparatively calm atmosphere with the Tyler administration were lost and the 1845 presidential election was won by an unknown westerner, James K. Polk. Polk had fought his campaign on the slogan '54° 40' or fight'. His Inaugural Speech left the world in no doubt that he intended the speedy incorporation of both Texas and the whole of the Oregon territory in the United States. The British government was sufficiently alarmed to begin to take military precautions **(16)**. Aberdeen spoke with unwonted firmness in the Lords, telling the House that no one would make greater sacrifices than he would to maintain peace: 'But our honour is a substantial property that we can never neglect . . . we possess rights which, in our opinion, are clear and unquestionable; and, by the blessing of God, and with your support, these rights we are fully prepared to maintain.' He sat down amidst 'loud and general applause'.

Fortunately the Americans were not so bellicose as their speeches suggested. James Buchanan, the new Secretary of State, suggested that a settlement might be found on 'the principle of give and take'. Negotiations took place in Washington; agreement was not reached until June 1846 when the territory was divided along the 49th parallel but with a diversion to allow the whole of Vancouver Island to remain British. The British claim to some of the disputed territory south of the 49th paralled was probably stronger than their claim to any territory renounced in the north-east boundary dispute but in the last resort the Americans cared about the disputed territory and had settlers to put into it, the British were still mainly concerned with a general settlement and comparatively indifferent to details. Even in the spring of 1846 an outbreak of hostilities had not seemed impossible, although the writer, J. W. Croker, was probably being unusually alarmist when he wrote to Aberdeen:

> ... for God's sake, end it: for if anything were to happen to Louis Philippe, we shall have an American war immediately, and a French one just after, a rebellion in Ireland, real starvation in the manufacturing districts, and a twenty per-cent complication in the shape of Income Tax.

Croker's gloomy prophecy illustrates the fact that all had not gone smoothly with the restoration of good relations with France either. The overt quarrel about the Eastern Question had been resolved by the Straits Convention of July 1841. Louis Philippe still felt too insecure on the throne of France and in his acceptance by the conservative eastern powers to wish for bad relations with England. Queen Victoria's private visit to the French royal family at the Château d'Eu in September 1843 (repeated in September 1845) was extremely gratifying to him and seemed to mark a new intimacy between the powers. François Guizot, who was both Prime Minister and Foreign Minister from 1841 to 1848, was a calm, scholarly man who proved to be a congenial colleague to Aberdeen (36). Indeed Peel worried, not without reason, how far good relations between the two powers were becoming dependent on the personal compatibility of the two foreign ministers. Outwardly relations had improved greatly and the period 1841–46 has not infrequently been referred to as the 'first *entente cordiale*' between those two traditionally antagonistic powers, Britain and France. But beneath the surface serious tensions remained (29, 42).

British and French parties still competed for influence in Greece and Spain. Three parties had emerged in Greece where King Otto had still not granted a constitution as promised by the three guarantor powers, Britain, France and Russia, but was ruling incompetently with the help of Bavarian friends. The Greeks were also in deep financial difficulties and frequently unable to pay the charges on the loan guaranteed by the three powers in 1832. Metaxa led a pro-Russian party which would not have been sorry to depose Otto and replace him by an Orthodox prince. Mavrocordato led the pro-British party and Coletti, who had been Greek ambassador in Paris and was a friend of Guizot, the French. The French had shown themselves more accomodating than the other powers about Greece's financial problems and the British suspected that this was merely intended to establish French influence. In September 1843 a revolution, headed by the army, took place and the rebels demanded a constitution. Aberdeen wrote to Peel: 'I am no lover of Revolutions. . . . But in truth, it is only the fulfilment of promises made by the three Powers, and by the King, many years ago' (36). In the cordial aftermath of the Château d'Eu meeting, the British and the French managed for some months to cooperate in Greece while a new constitution was drawn up. Mavrocordato became prime minister but in the summer of 1844 Coletti and Metaxa cooperated to bring down Mavrocordato's government. Aberdeen while maintaining that it was 'a matter of supreme indifference' to him who was prime minister of Greece and instructing the British Minister in Athens, Admiral Lyons, that it was no part of his duties to strive for British influence, felt betrayed by the French. He was unable to alter the situation and some time later, at the time of the Don Pacifico affair, Palmerston was convinced that the trouble had begun under Aberdeen when proper British influence was not maintained in Greece.

In Spain too Aberdeen insisted that he did not want to maintain any particular 'British' party. The civil war had finally ended in 1839 with the victory of the government forces under General Espartero and the exile of Carlos. Espartero, however, had allied his fortunes with the Radicals (the *Progresistas*) and when in 1840 Queen Christina tried to get rid of him, she was forced to flee to France and Espartero became Regent in her stead (78). In July 1843 Espartero was in turn overthrown and in November the thirteen-year-old Queen Isabella was declared to be of age to obviate the need for a Regency. This made more urgent a question already under discussion, that of the marriages of Isabella and her younger sister, the Infanta Louisa Fernanda.

There was no shortage of candidates. The British would have been pleased to see the choice fall on a Saxe-Coburg prince, Leopold, the Prince Consort's cousin, but the only candidates they really objected to were the sons of Louis-Philippe. Aberdeen and Guizot reached an informal agreement at the first Château d'Eu meeting that both Leopold and the Orleanist princes should be excluded as suitors for Isabella. Metternich favoured the son of Don Carlos but this did not meet with British or French approval. Other possible candidates, all Bourbons, included the comte de Trapani, the brother of the King of Naples, and Isabella's two Spanish cousins, the Dukes of Cadiz and Seville. Aberdeen maintained throughout that the matter was really one for the Spaniards and Guizot at least affected to despise these dynastic considerations – this affair straight out of Shakespeare and the Middle Ages, as he once called it. At the second Château d'Eu meeting, in September 1845, Aberdeen indicated (although Peel subsequently disapproved) that once Isabella was married and had children, Britain would not see insuperable objections to her sister marrying an Orleanist prince [doc. 41]. The Coburg candidature was revived in Spain in the winter of 1845–46, although without any official British backing. Guizot was moved to communicate a memorandum to the French Ambassador in London on 27 February 1846, clearly indicating that if there was any possibility of either Isabella or her sister marrying a prince who was not a descendant of Philip V (that is, a Bourbon) he would feel himself freed from any engagements not to press for an Orleanist marriage. The importance of this only became apparent after the fall of Peel's government (21, 70).

Greece and Spain illustrate the difficulties of Britain and France keeping in step in this period but the major difficulties were to arise elsewhere. In 1829 Charles X had launched an attack on Algiers to free the Mediterranean from the Barbary pirates who still molested trade, incredible though it may seem, in the middle of the nineteenth century. Charles himself had fallen from power the following year and the Orleanist government had inherited the legacy of a French foothold in Algeria. They would gladly have relinquished it but for prestige reasons dared not; they found themselves drawn deeper and deeper into the hinterland and in the 1840s Marshal Bugeaud conducted a major campaign to subdue the whole country. The British had never liked the French presence in Algeria but accorded it grudging acquiescence so long as it was not extended to Algeria's neighbours, Tunis and Morocco. In the middle of 1844, however, a dispute between France and Morocco led to the former power bombarding Tangiers. This extension of the North African conflict was very seriously regarded in Britain (42). It was taken the more gravely because it coincided with a serious Anglo-French clash in the Pacific.

France, like Britain, had been interested in the Pacific in the 1780s. Captain Phillip had taken possession of Botany Bay in 1788 only just ahead of a projected French expedition. But the French Revolution and the Napoleonic wars had almost extinguished French interest in the area. It had revived in the 1830s. The Pope had established the Apostolic Vicariate of the Pacific in 1833 and Catholic missions had gone out under French patronage. The July Monarchy was interested in the acquisition of naval and mercantile stations in the Pacific. A private French company was interested in the colonisation of New

Zealand but was beaten to the draw by the British, who annexed New Zealand in 1840. This action caused considerable indignation in France and when in 1842 Admiral Dupetit-Thouars proclaimed a protectorate over Tahiti it was openly welcomed as a 'tit-for-tat' in France. It was very unwelcome in Britain where Tahiti had long been considered 'almost an English island' with British traders and missionaries well established. The British grudgingly acquiesced in the protectorate but the trouble became much more acute two years later in the summer of 1844 when the French annexed the island and imprisoned a leading British missionary, George Pritchard, who was also the British consul. Every nerve, trading interests, religious zeal, the defence of diplomatic immunity, had been touched [doc. 40]. Public excitement became difficult to control and for a short time Britain and France were close to war, but Aberdeen and Guizot refused to be rattled and gradually tempers cooled and compromises were found (36, 42).

Nevertheless, after the summer of 1844 many, including Peel and Wellington, feared that the French *entente* was hollow. Peel had always had less faith in it than Aberdeen [doc. 39]. He and Wellington began to look instead to the strengthening of Britain's defences. A new factor had now entered the situation, the increasing importance of steam navigation. One of Louis-Philippe's younger sons, the Prince de Joinville, had just published a monumentally tactless pamphlet, explaining how the British navy could be decoyed away while a fleet of French steamships, no longer dependent on wind and tide, could slip across the Channel in a few hours and land an invading army. This was exactly what British strategists feared and Wellington wrote alarming reports to the effect that nowhere on the south coast, except the beach immediately under Dover Castle, was adequately defended against such attacks. To Aberdeen this was the negation of all he had striven for. He argued that nothing was more false than Wellington's contention, *para bellum, pacem habebis* (if you would have peace, prepare for war) and offered his resignation. Peel refused to accept it but continued during the last years of his administration to pursue his conciliatory policies while co-operating with Wellington in looking to Britain's defences [doc. 36].

The crisis with France in the summer of 1844 led Peel and Aberdeen to seek a closer understanding with Russia. The Tsar came on a well publicised visit to London, during which he made a theatrical offer to Victoria that all his forces were at her disposal in any war with France. More seriously he wished to discuss the future of the Turkish empire. There is unfortunately no exactly contemporary record of what was said between the Tsar, Peel and Aberdeen in the intervals between formal engagements, but the Tsar took it sufficiently seriously on his return to Russia to send Nesselrode to London to get the agreement put into writing [doc. 48]. Both powers agreed that their first objective should be to preserve the integrity of the Turkish empire but if, unhappily, the empire collapsed they would consult on their course of action. It is difficult to know whether Peel or Aberdeen attached much significance to this document at the time or whether they regarded it as an anodyne statement of good intentions, but it was to assume much greater importance eight years later in the preliminaries to the Crimean war (53, 75).

In June 1846 Peel's government fell as the result of the repeal of the Corn Laws. Lord John Russell succeeded as Prime Minister and Palmerston returned to the Foreign Office. The latter was not a foregone conclusion; when Peel had resigned and Russell had tried to form an administration the previous December, opposition within the Whig party to Palmerston returning to the Foreign Office had been so strong that Russell had failed to form a government. Palmerston was sufficiently worried to go to France at Easter 1846 and engage in an ostentatious reconciliation with his former opponents, including Guizot (13).

Immediately Palmerston returned to office, another Anglo-French incident arose over the Spanish marriage question. Aberdeen had briefed Palmerston on the current state of foreign affairs before leaving office but Palmerston had perhaps failed to realise the delicacy of the Spanish question. In his first despatch to Henry Bulwer, the British Minister in Madrid, Palmerston named the possible candidates for the queen's hand and included Leopold [doc. 41]. So little did he regard this as a breach of faith with France that he showed the despatch to the French representative in London, the comte de Jarnac. Guizot immediately saw the opportunity to escape from previous engagements and, perhaps, to revenge himself on Palmerston for his previous slights of France. On 10 October 1846 Queen Isabella was married to her cousin, the Duke of Cadiz, and immediately afterwards, her sister was married to a younger son of Louis-Philippe, the duc de Montpensier. Metternich, who was anxious to be on good terms with Guizot's conservative government, declined to join Palmerston in any protest. At the time it was widely believed that the marriage between Isabella and Cadiz would prove infertile, but Isabella had several children so no question of a possible union of the French and Spanish thrones ever materialised. The affair caused a profound coldness between London and Paris and the French government, unable to cooperate effectively any more with Britain, aligned itself increasingly with the policy of the three eastern powers (20, 70).

The years after 1846 were dominated by disastrous harvests and revolutionary outbreaks all over Europe, culminating in the widespread disruptions of 1848. Palmerston gained a popular reputation as the staunch and successful defender of liberal causes. In fact, he was very cautious in his support of revolutions, not only because his guiding principle was always British interests (although that was the case) but also because he felt sympathy only for the most moderate and 'constitutional' of them and the number of occasions on which he was able to intervene successfully were very few [doc. 42].

The first troubles occurred in Poland. The Treaty of Vienna had declared Cracow to be a free city under the joint protection of Russia, Prussia and Austria but in February 1846 the Poles in Austrian Poland (Galicia) rose and were joined by the people of Cracow in demanding a free and independent Poland. The rising was suppressed by Austrian troops and in November 1846 the three eastern powers agreed that Cracow should be incorporated into Austria. Britain and France protested separately at this breach of the Treaty of Vienna but they were unable to concert their policy because of the estrangement arising from the Spanish marriage question. But even together the two powers could have done nothing against a *fait accompli* since neither was in the least prepared to resort to military force (20, 78).

Palmerston was rather more successful in Portugal. When the general election of 1845 returned a large majority for the radical Septembrist party, Queen Maria annulled the constitution and appointed Marshal Saldanha as dictator. Civil war seemed a real possibility and the Queen appealed to the signatories of the 1834 Quadruple Alliance. Palmerston, to the irritation of Victoria, expressed some public approval for the Septembrists. Guizot and the Spanish government were anxious to intervene on Maria's side. On this occasion Palmerston worked with considerable skill for a tripartite intervention which, although it led to the surrender of the Septembrists' army, compelled Maria to restore the constitution (20, 78).

In Switzerland Palmerston gained a reputation for the support of liberalism which was only partly deserved. Here the quarrel was between the liberal, centralising, Protestant cantons and the conservative, Catholic cantons (the *Sonderbund*), who were deeply attached to cantonal rights, even when this meant the perpetuation of old abuses such as the use of torture in judicial proceedings. Both Metternich and Guizot wished to support the *Sonderbund*, even to the extent of armed intervention. Palmerston sympathised with the Protestant cantons and employed diplomatic delaying tactics on their behalf (20), but he was not, as was popularly supposed, the instigator of the Protestant attack on Fribourg in November 1847, which left them in a commanding military position at the beginning of the winter of 1847–48. In fact, he had counselled against such action. Palmerston, who certainly did not mean to carry the Swiss question to the length of war, would have been powerless if France and Austria, possibly joined by Prussia, had backed the *Sonderbund* in the spring of 1848. He was saved from facing such a dilemma by the revolutions which broke out in Paris, Vienna and Berlin in February and March 1848 (78).

The revolution in France began on 23 February 1848 and the following day Louis-Philippe abdicated and the Second Republic was proclaimed. Louis-Philippe and Guizot fled to England, where Palmerston received them courteously enough. He was not sorry to see the end of Guizot's government for not only had Guizot played him what he regarded as a dirty trick over the Spanish marriages, he was also quietly aligning his policy with that of Metternich and leaving Britain isolated on questions such as the *Sonderbund* (20) [doc. 43]. Palmerston did, however, feel some anxiety at the end of constitutional monarchy in France. Lamartine formed a provisional government which included not only representatives of the disaffected middle classes but also socialists such as Louis Blanc. Thirty years earlier this might have been held to be a clear case for action under the Quadruple Alliance, a revolutionary government in Paris which might well threaten the order of all Europe, but two of the eastern powers were paralysed by their own revolutions and Palmerston preferred to support Lamartine's government lest it be replaced by a more extreme body. He believed 'the only hope for the maintenance of internal tranquillity, and for the permanent restoration of order in France, lies in the continuance, for the present at least, of M. Lamartine and his Colleagues in Power' (7). The only reassurance he insisted on was that the French would not engage in an aggressive foreign policy. On this Lamartine's famous circular despatch of 7 March was ambiguous: by it France refused to recognise the validity of the Vienna Settlement but expressed her intention of living in peace with all nations. Palmerston chose to attach more importance to the latter than to the former; at the same time he lamented the 'inherent aggressiveness' of republics and feared that the spectacle of universal suffrage being granted in France would stir up trouble in England. Palmerston was no friend of the further extension of the franchise and, although Britain was to escape the revolutions which afflicted continental Europe, the government was for a time seriously alarmed by the Chartist agitation culminating in the intended march on Parliament in April 1848.

Italy was the severest test of Palmerston's statemanship in this period. Revolution in Italy actually preceded that in France and European conservatives even suspected Palmerston of having stirred up the trouble himself. Their suspicions centred on a special mission to Rome which Palmerston had entrusted to an old friend, Lord Minto, in 1847. Minto had gone with instructions to encourage the new Pope, Pius IX, to continue his mildly reforming policy in order to avert revolution and to try to persuade the Pope, first, to discourage rebellion in Ireland (which was still in ferment after the potato famine of 1846) and, secondly, to recall the Jesuits from Switzerland, which would have removed one major cause of controversy between the Protestant and Catholic cantons. The Austrians were, however, extremely sensitive about Italy and had already used their treaty rights to send an army to Ferrara in July 1847 (78).

Widespread unrest in Italy in 1847 culminated in January 1848 when a successful rising in Palermo compelled the King of Naples, Ferdinand II, to grant his people a constitution, and when the people of Milan demonstrated against the heavy Austrian tax on tobacco, the so-called 'Smoking Riots'. By March Austrian-controlled Lombardy and Venetia were in revolt. On 23 March Charles Albert, the king of Piedmont-Sardinia, after many hesitations, decided to throw in his lot with Italian nationalism and declared war on Austria. Naples, Tuscany and Parma and Modena made common cause with Sardinia. Pope Pius IX, who had become the hero of many Italians for his earlier reforms, could not however bring himself to support Italian nationalism against Austria and, after further domestic struggles in Naples, Ferdinand II withdrew his support for Sardinia in May.

Palmerston, like many Englishmen of his class, had some genuine sympathy for Italian nationalism but his policy was determined more by a hard-headed calculation of British interests. He was most concerned about the balance of power in Europe and this led him to certain conclusions, from which he never fundamentally departed for the rest of his career. Austria must be maintained as a great power to balance the strength of Russia in the Balkans and eastern Europe, but in order to do this effectively Austria must concentrate her strength north of the Alps and disentangle herself from what Palmerston regarded as her over-commitment in Italy. The problem in Italy was, as A.J.P. Taylor puts it, to get Austria out, without letting the French in: a power vacuum in Italy was bound to be a temptation to the Second Republic (87, 88) [doc. 44].

Palmerston played his part skilfully but cautiously. He was certainly not able to dictate events as some of his admirers supposed, but the

French were equally hesitant and the Italians were deeply divided among themselves about both objectives and methods. The Austrian general, Radetzky, defeated Charles Albert at Custozza on 25 July 1848 and an armistice was arranged, but all did not yet seem lost for the Italian cause. Palmerston still hoped that he might be able to secure Lombardy for Sardinia and some form of home rule for Venice, that ancient republic whose independence had only been ended by the Napoleonic wars. Palmerston suggested joint Anglo-French mediation and reluctantly agreed to an international conference (which never in fact met) to guard against any unilateral French action. The war between Sardinia and Austria was resumed in March 1849 but it was too late for the Italians. Order had been restored in other parts of the empire and Austria had largely regained her strength. On 23 March Radetzky decisively defeated Charles Albert at Novara and Charles Albert subsequently abdicated in favour of his son, Victor Emmanuel. On 27 August Venice, where a republic had been proclaimed by Manin the previous year, surrendered to the Austrians. The Pope had fled from Rome in November 1848 and in February 1849 a republic had been proclaimed there too. The Pope asked for the support of the powers to restore his territories to him. Austria, France and Naples all responded. Mazzini and Garibaldi defended Rome until 3 June 1849 when French troops entered the city. The *status quo* appeared to have been restored throughout Italy. If Palmerston's objectives had been, as European conservatives supposed, to support Italian nationalism, he would have been decisively defeated, but this objective existed almost entirely in their imaginations. Palmerston had largely succeeded in his much more limited objective of ensuring that no settlement should be reached which would be seriously inimical to British interests (**78, 87**).

If mild sympathy was the warmest feeling Palmerston entertained for Italian nationalism, even that was lacking in his attitude to German nationalism (**13**). He showed very little either understanding of, or interest in events in Germany in 1848–49. The only aspect in which he became directly involved was the Schleswig-Holstein question. The Duchies of Schleswig and Holstein were united to Denmark by a personal union similar to that between Britain and Hanover, but since the Salic Law, which forbade succession through the female line, applied in the Duchies but not in Denmark, separation would occur on the death of the childless Prince Frederick, then heir to the Danish throne, just as the link between England and Hanover had been broken when Victoria succeeded to the British throne. There were Danes in both Duchies, although Holstein was predominantly German and a member of the German Confederation. Just before the revolutions of 1848 the Danes tried to incorporate the Duchies into Denmark. This angered the German-speakers in the Duchies and they appealed to the new liberal parliament at Frankfurt, which the revolution in Germany had just brought into existence. The Frankfurt parliament and the new liberal government in Prussia supported the Germans in the Duchies and declared war on Denmark. Russia came out in support of the Danish king. Palmerston was solely concerned to prevent a European war and he persuaded both sides to submit the dispute to an international conference in London – on the lines of the conference which had once sat on Belgian affairs – over which he presided. Various compromises were suggested but rejected by one side or the other. Eventually in May 1852 Denmark and the powers signed a treaty in London which settled the succession to both Denmark and the Duchies on Prince Christian of Glucksbourg. Duke Christian of Augustenburg, who would have succeeded to the Duchies under the Salic Law, was persuaded to renounce his claim (23).

Palmerston's desire to see Austria continue as a great power led him in to a very ambiguous attitude towards the revolution in Hungary. [doc. 45] On the one hand he sympathised with the aristocratic leaders of the Hungarian revolt. He felt that they were reasserting Hungary's ancient rights as a kingdom and, in a letter to Lord John Russell, compared them with the English 'revolutionists' of 1688. If Palmerston did not appreciate that the Hungarians, while claiming their own national rights, were vigorously suppressing the national claims of the Slavs within their frontiers, he was no more ignorant than practically everybody else in western Europe at the time (78). But his fears of the disintegration of the Austrian empire were so great that he almost welcomed the intervention of Russian troops, at Austria's request, finally to extinguish the Hungarian revolt in July 1849 (83, 84).

European conservatives saw Palmerston as the villain of the piece in 1848–49, constantly succouring revolutionary causes. In fact he did no such thing. The balance of power meant more to him than nationalism and he was under no illusions that what was going on in Europe was not merely a struggle for constitutional rights, of which he might approve, but a great social upheaval which might lead no man knew where. He wrote to the British Minister in Munich as early as 20 April 1848: 'The Struggle now going on in many parts of Europe is one between those who have no property and those who wish to keep it.' At the same time the more the conservatives denounced him, the more British liberals and radicals hailed him as their hero. When German conservatives wrathfully made up the doggerel, *'Hat der Teufel einen Sohn, so ist er sicher Palmerston'* British Liberals approvingly translated it 'If the devil has a son, his name is surely Palmerston'. For the first time in his life Palmerston was thoroughly popular with the British electorate and he to some extent played up to it by his quite blunt public statements about the shortcomings of the autocracies of Europe (78).

All this helped to estrange Palmerston from the Court. Victoria had not liked his recognition of the Second Republic in France and she may have believed some of the exaggerated suspicions of European royalties as to Palmerston's radicalism. She and Albert certainly exaggerated the anti-Austrian nature of Palmerston's policy. Two incidents, in themselves trivial, aggravated the situation. In 1850 the Austrian General Haynau, who had been responsible for some savage reprisals against the rebels in both Italy and Hungary, came to London. When he visited Barclay's Brewery in Southwark, a tourist sight of the time, he was set upon by the draymen and beaten up. Privately, Palmerston seems to have considered the incident a good joke and well deserved. He angered Victoria by refusing at first to send anything like what she considered an adequate explanation and apology to the Austrian government. The following year the Hungarian nationalist leader, Kossuth, visited England and was treated to a hero's welcome. Palmerston was only reluctantly dissuaded from seeing him by Victoria and various Cabinet colleagues. Victoria made no secret of the fact that she would have liked to have seen him leave the Foreign Office (25) but he was first to score a great parliamentary success.

Some Polish and Hungarian refugees had fled to Turkey. The Russians and the Austrians brought heavy pressure to bear on the Sultan to surrender them. Palmerston sent a fleet to the eastern Mediterranean and persuaded the French to do likewise to give the Sultan moral support; the Russians and the Austrians then withdrew most of their demands (7). While the British fleet was still in the eastern Mediterranean, Palmerston thought of new employment for it. The result was the rather ludicrous Don Pacifico affair.

Don Pacifico was a Portuguese Jew, who claimed British citizenship on the grounds that he had been born in Gibraltar. At Easter 1847 his house in Athens was burnt down by an antisemitic mob. Having failed to get redress in other ways, Don Pacifico appealed to the British government. Palmerston was the more ready to listen because this was simply the latest in a long list of outrages against British subjects, for which the Greek government seemed unable or unwilling to provide redress. He protested strongly to the Greek government but nothing was done. In January 1850 the British squadron was sent to Piraeus, the port of

Athens, to establish a blockade until a number of British claims, including that of Don Pacifico, were met. The Greeks gave in but Britain's co-guarantors of Greece, Russia and France protested (78).

On 17 June 1850 the Conservative leader, Lord Stanley, moved a vote of censure on the government in the House of Lords for their conduct towards Greece and two days later the vote was carried by 169 to 132. Palmerston offered to resign but the Prime Minister, Lord John Russell, preferred to put the matter to the test of a debate in the Commons. The Commons debate extended over four days, from 24 to 28 June. It was a full dress attack on Palmerston's foreign policy. The Conservatives rallied all their forces to criticise Palmerston not only for the Don Pacifico affair but for his conduct throughout 1848 and 1849. Others, like Richard Cobden and William Gladstone, still a Peelite at this time, criticised Palmerston for the blustering nature of his foreign policy. In reply Palmerston made a comprehensive defence of his policy but he won the House and the public by his famous *Civis Romanus sum* passage [doc. 46]. The government won the vote of confidence by 310 to 246. Almost all the Radicals voted for him.

Palmerston seemed entrenched in power after the Don Pacifico debate but his independence of action was irritating both the Court and his Cabinet colleagues. Victoria continually complained that he sent off foreign despatches without her seeing them [doc. 47]. She even asked Russell to move him to some other office (25). Russell resisted the suggestions for some time but late in 1851 Palmerston committed an unexpected political blunder. On 2 December 1851 Louis Napoleon, Napoleon I's nephew who had been quite legally elected President of the Second Republic in December 1848, seized supreme power by a *coup d'état,* dissolving the National Assembly and arresting leading Republicans. Palmerston, in agreement with his cabinet colleagues, told the British Ambassador in Paris to maintain a neutral attitude but he incautiously told the French Ambassador in London that he was pleased by the *coup.* The matter leaked out and Russell asked for his resignation. What embarrassed Palmerston more, Russell made the whole incident public in the Commons. Palmerston, the hero of the Radicals, was revealed applauding an authoritarian *coup d'état*; many, including Benjamin Disraeli, thought that he was finished. Palmerston in fact retaliated with great skill. Napoleon's actions had revived British fears of Bonapartist aggression. Palmerston had long advocated that Britain's defences be put in order. When Russell's government introduced a Bill in the Commons in February 1852 to set up a county militia, he capped their proposals with an amendment that the militia should be organised on a national basis for greater efficiency: the amendment was carried and Russell resigned (78).

Lord Derby formed a Conservative administration and asked Palmerston to join it as Chancellor of the Exchequer. Palmerston declined but during the next eighteen months he carried on a political flirtation with the Conservatives (78). When Derby was finally defeated in December 1852 Aberdeen, with great difficulty, formed a coalition government of Whigs and Peelites (24). Palmerston consented to take the Home Office. Russell went briefly to the Foreign Office but was succeeded in February 1853 by the Earl of Clarendon. Clarendon had begun his professional life as a diplomat, serving in St Petersburg and Madrid, and had been Lord Lieutenant of Ireland from 1847 to 1852, but he made little impact on British foreign policy (63). He remained in office until 1858, but always behind him stood two more powerful figures, Palmerston and Aberdeen.

Although Palmerston and Aberdeen had by now come to stand in popular estimation for two quite different schools of foreign policy, neither man thought it impossible to cooperate with the other in 1852. Aberdeen himself told the House of Lords in December 1852: 'Though there may have been differences in the execution, according to the different hands entrusted with the direction of affairs, the principles of the foreign policy of the country have, for the last thirty years, been the same.' In domestic affairs the Coalition worked together better than had been expected from its difficult beginning and it might have been the same in foreign affairs if the Eastern Question had not erupted into one of its periodic bouts of activity.

The Eastern Question had been comparatively quiescent since 1841. British attempts to induce the Ottoman empire to reform itself, conducted through their ambassador in Constantinople, Stratford Canning, later Lord Stratford de Redcliffe, had failed (92). The immediate antecedent to the Crimean war was the dispute about the care of the Holy Places. Both Catholic and Orthodox Christians claimed rights and privileges in the Holy Places in Jerusalem and elsewhere. Catholic rights had been confirmed by the Turks in 1740 but they had been allowed to fall into disuse while Orthodox claims had been exercised and even extended. In 1850 Louis Napoleon, desiring to please the French Catholics, took up the question of Catholic rights with the Porte. The Russian government pressed counterclaims for the Orthodox Christians. The Holy Places dispute itself was settled in May 1853 through the good offices of Lord Stratford but by then the atmosphere had become embittered. In February 1853 the Tsar sent Prince Menshikov on a special mission to Constantinople to reassert Orthodox claims and to threaten a breach of diplomatic relations if Russian terms were not met. Menshikov was a soldier, not a diplomat, and he had instructions to adopt a high tone with the Turks. He secured the resignation of Fuad Pasha, the Turkish Foreign Minister, who was disliked by the Russians, but he failed to obtain his more far-reaching demands. The Russians suspected that this was due to the influence of Stratford. Aberdeen and Clarendon were themselves doubtful of the suitability of Stratford remaining at Constantinople but they left him there. In fact on a number of occasions during the crisis Stratford exerted a pacifying influence and there is no direct evidence that he persuaded the Turks to reject Menshikov's proposals, which were in any case unacceptable to them (5, 59).

The Russian response to Turkey's rejection of the Menshikov mission was to occupy the Principalities of Moldavia and Wallachia, where she retained treaty rights from the Treaty of Adrianople of 1829. On 30 May 1853 the British Cabinet authorised Stratford to summon the British Mediterranean fleet to Constantinople if he thought it necessary. In the middle of June the British fleet moved to Besika Bay, just outside the Dardanelles, where they were joined by a French fleet. None of the great powers desired war but they were all beginning to use their armies and fleets as dangerous counters in the diplomatic game (5).

The Russians hoped to be able to count on Austria as an ally in return for their help in suppressing the Hungarians in 1849 but the Austrians were very hesitant and halfhearted in their support of Russia. In fact the Russian occupation of the Principalities at the mouth of the Danube inconvenienced them more than it did the Turks. Late in July the Austrian Foreign Minister, Count Buol, in consultation with the British and French Ambassadors, put forward a peace proposal, the Vienna Note. The Sultan was to promise to observe his existing treaties of Kuchuk Kainardji (1774) and Adrianople (1829) with Russia, confirming the rights of the Orthodox Church; to extend to Orthodox Christians any privileges enjoyed by other Christian denominations; and to make no changes in the position of his Christian subjects without the agreement of France and Russia. The Russian government accepted the Vienna Note in August. But in the meantime the Turks on Stratford's advice had drawn up an alternative and less far-reaching proposal which, rather unfortunately, became known as the 'Turkish ultimatum'. The Turks refused to accept the Vienna Note unless it was made clear that any privileges enjoyed by Orthodox Christians stemmed from the Sultan's will and not from treaties with Russia. The Russians refused to accept either the Turkish ultimatum or the proposed modification of the Vienna Note. The situation became worse when in September a Berlin newspaper secured a copy of a memorandum by Nesselrode making it clear that the Russians interpreted the Vienna Note as giving them a general right of intervention in the Ottoman empire on behalf of Orthodox Christians. This so-called 'violent interpretation' was quite contrary to the British and French understanding of the Note (5).

The British government was experiencing the utmost difficulty in formulating a consistent policy. Their suspicions had been aroused by some conversations between the Tsar and the British Ambassador, Sir George Hamilton Seymour, as early as January 1853 [doc. 49]. The Tsar, who was deeply distrustful of France, had apparently decided to open discussions with England even before he was sure that Aberdeen was coming back into office but Aberdeen's return seems to have persuaded him that he could take matters up where he left them off in 1844. The 1844 conversations had always been taken much more seriously in St Petersburg than in London. Seymour may have inadvertently encouraged him for when the Tsar expressed his pleasure at Aberdeen's return, Seymour took the opportunity to bring up the question of Turkey. The Tsar was at first cautious, speaking of Turkey as a 'sick man' (the famous 'sick bear' reference came a little later) and the desirability of Britain and Russia coming to a 'good understanding'. It was not until nearly a month later that the Tsar began to suggest the possible divisions of the Turkish empire if it in fact collapsed. The British replied that they thought collapse was still a long way off. When the record of the Seymour conversations and Nesselrode's memorandum of 1844 [doc. 48] were laid before Parliament in 1854 they seemed to suggest a clear sequence of events with the Tsar plotting the disemberment of the Turkish empire, which helped to excite public opinion. Nothing could have been further from the truth but the Tsar's belief that he had some kind of understanding with Aberdeen and that England, under Aberdeen, would not go to war with Russia, led him to disregard other plain warnings (5, 24, 44).

The British Cabinet was divided although they had no illusions about the potential seriousness of the situation. As early as May 1853 Aberdeen had foreseen that the problem might lead to a European war, although he was determined to prevent it if possible. But on 23 September Clarendon, with Aberdeen's consent, ordered Stratford to bring the British fleet up to Constantinople in view of the deteriorating situation. Stratford, moving with extreme caution, did not actually summon the fleet until 20 October. One of the most crucial Cabinet meetings was that of 7 October: Palmerston proposed that Britain should not only promise the Turks naval assistance but should send the British fleet into the Black Sea to detain any Russian ships cruising there; such a proposal was obviously tantamount to war. The majority of the Cabinet, Aberdeen, Clarendon, the Duke of Argyll, Sidney Herbert, Charles Wood, Lord Granville and, a little hesitantly, the Duke of Newcastle were still for seeking a peaceful solution. At this time only Palmerston, Russell and Lord Lansdowne were bellicose (24), but the balance in the Cabinet gradually shifted. Palmerston converted Clarendon to a strong line and Clarendon's conversion swayed the younger men, including even Gladstone. Eventually Aberdeen was left isolated in his own Cabinet. Palmerston's latest biographer suggests that, in order to counter Aberdeen's appeasement, he urged Aberdeen to stronger action than he would himself have taken if he had been in charge of affairs 'and he certainly made more provocative speeches about Russia in the House of Commons than he usually did when he was handling a critical international situation' (78).

Public opinion in the form of virulent Russophobia was becoming a factor in the situation. Russia had been unpopular with the British public since the 1830s, partly because of Poland, partly because of fears of Russia's growing naval strength, which were first voiced in the mid-thirties. The Russian intervention in Hungary in 1849 had intensified these feelings. Some men were also beginning to see Russia as a potential threat to Britain's Indian empire and so as a greater threat than the traditional enemy, France (35). The press was generally anti-Russian in tone and numerous anti-Russian pamphlets circulated, some of the most extreme but also the most persuasive being the work of David Urquhart, a former diplomat who was wild enough to believe that Palmerston himself was in the Russian pay (89). The precarious nature of the Aberdeen coalition made it particularly difficult for it to resist the pressure of public opinion, especially when it found echoes in Parliament (62).

The so-called 'massacre' of Sinope set light to the tinder. The Russians and the Turks had drifted into war in the first week of October and some land fighting had already taken place when, on 30 November 1853, the Russian Black Sea fleet sank a Turkish squadron in the harbour of Sinope. It was a legitimate act of war and, despite allegations that the Russians had continued to fire after the Turks had ceased to resist, there were no real grounds for the British press denouncing it as 'an act of barbarism'. Palmerston had resigned from the Cabinet on 14 December, not at least ostensibly on a question of foreign policy but because he disapproved of Russell's proposals for the extension of the franchise. He rejoined the Cabinet on 24 December. Even without Palmerston, the Cabinet was finding it difficult to resist the demands for action: they were further moved by the belief that the French would act if they did not. Napoleon was reported to be determined to 'sweep the Black Sea of the Russian flag'. A Cabinet meeting of 22 December agreed to order the British fleet into the Black Sea.

The British and French fleets entered the Black Sea on 3 January 1854. The Russians asked whether the fleets had instructions to restrain the Turks as well as the Russians. When they did not receive assurances on this they withdrew their ambassadors from London and Paris. Late in February the two western powers asked the Russians for an assurance that they would evacuate Moldavia and Wallachia by the end of April. Receiving no reply to this, Britain and France declared war on Russia on 28 March 1854 (5).

They had not concerted their policy with Austria or Prussia, who both remained neutral. On 3 June the Austrians demanded on their own account that the Russians should evacuate the Principalities. The Russians reluctantly agreed to do so in return for an Austrian promise that she would prevent Britain and France from occupying them, and the Russian forces were accordingly withdrawn and replaced by Austrian troops. This had important implications for the Anglo-French plan of campaign. Their first care had been to protect the Dardanelles and Constantinople itself from any fears of a Russian attack and this had been accomplished without difficulty. Forces had then been moved to Varna to help the Turkish forces regain the Principalities and to prevent a Russian advance from the Danube. But the effective neutralisation of the Principalities in the charge of Austria meant that this was no longer a theatre of war. The Allies then turned to a scheme which had been discussed in the British Cabinet as early as January 1854, to attack the great Russian naval base of Sevastopol and so end her maritime predominance in the Black Sea. The war thus became concentrated on the Crimea (5, 24).

The Crimean War was fought in a blaze of publicity compared with earlier campaigns. W.H. Russell of *The Times* was the first really modern war correspondent, who kept his paper supplied with vivid and highly critical accounts, which were not subjected to the censorship to which they would have been liable in later wars. The new art of photography was employed for the first time to reveal war scenes to the public. The inefficiency of both the commissariat and the medical services could not long escape public attention. More men died of disease than by enemy action and Florence Nightingale became a national heroine for her attempts to organise the base hospital at Scutari.

Despite the deficiencies of their high commands the allied forces were not without military successes. They effected their landing in the

Crimea in September 1854 and defeated Menshikov at the battle of Alma on 20 September but they delayed for a fatal three weeks before laying siege to Sevastopol itself, thus giving the Russians time to organise its defences. The battles of Balaclava on 25 October and of Inkerman on 5 November were qualified successes for the Allies. They prevented the Russians from relieving Sevastopol but, by their famous charge at Balaclava, the Light Brigade lost two-thirds of their strength in twenty minutes, and at Inkerman the Allies lost so many men that they could no longer hope to take Sevastopol by assault and were committed to wintering in the Crimea – a possibility no one had envisaged at the beginning of the campaign. Their position was made much worse when on 14 November a great storm wrecked the British transport ships.

Public opinion was beginning to change. There were still those who looked on the war as a crusade against Tsarist tyranny. Some even argued that the fires of war would be a blessing to England herself, burning out the dross of a materialist civilisation and uniting the people who had been bitterly divided by the traumas of the new industrialised society. The poet laureate, Tennyson, summed this up in rather bad verse [doc. 50]. But others began to be impressed by the arguments of Richard Cobden and John Bright who had consistently opposed the war. Cobden deliberately eschewed emotionalism and continually asked his countrymen for what purpose the war was being fought and what good it could possibly achieve. [doc. 51] (44).

The Times wrote on 23 January 1855·

> The deadlock is absolute, final, inevitable, and desperate, from White-hall to the camp before Sebastopol. The Minister of War, the Commander-in-Chief at home, the Commander-in-Chief in the Crimea, down to the purveyor of stores at Scutari, and the miserable lad dozing, naked and frostbitten in the trench are all equally dummies.

The same day the radical, Roebuck, gave notice in the Commons of a motion to set up a committee of enquiry into the conduct of the war. The following day Lord John Russell resigned from the government. On 25 January Roebuck's motion was carried by 305 votes to 157. Aberdeen's government resigned.

5 Lord Palmerston as Prime Minister

After Derby and Russell had both failed to form a government, the Queen turned reluctantly to Palmerston. Palmerston was popular in the country and acceptable to Parliament. Disraeli might scoff at him as 'an old painted pantaloon' but Palmerston knew, as he wrote to his brother, 'I am, for the moment, *l'inévitable'*. Although he was now over seventy years of age he threw himself with great energy into the conduct of the war (78).

The Crimean War has been described as 'a series of negotiations, punctuated by battles' and there is truth in this witticism. The war dragged on. In January 1855 Sardinia joined the Allies. Britain and France were glad to accept the 15,000 troops which Sardinia sent to the Crimea, although the French insisted that Sardinia must be promised no support against Austria in Italy in return. To the western powers the support of Austria was much more crucial than that of Sardinia if they were to bring the war to a successful conclusion. The Austrians were not entirely deaf to western overtures. Although they had persuaded the Russians to evacuate the Principalities, they still feared that Russian hostility might be turned on them and they wanted the war to end as quickly as possible. Negotiations between the Austrians and the French resulted in the formulation of four aims (the Four Points) agreed by Austria, France and Britain. Russia was to renounce her special rights in the Principalities and in Serbia. There was to be free navigation of the Danube. The Straits Convention of 1841 was to be revised 'in the interests of the Balance of Power in Europe'. Finally, Russia was to renounce her claims to a protectorate over the Orthodox Christians of the Ottoman empire. At the end of November 1854 Nicholas reluctantly accepted the Four Points as a basis for negotiations but by this time a firmer understanding had been reached between Britain, France, Austria, and Prussia. The Prussians had guaranteed the Austrian forces in the Principalities against a Russian attack and the French had guaranteed the Austrian position in Italy. On 2 December, Austria, Britain and France signed an alliance for the defence of the Principalities (5, 44).

Public excitement in Britain encouraged the British government to press for a much more severe interpretation of the third point than had originally been envisaged (44). They now wished to end Russian hegemony in the Black Sea by destroying Sevastopol as a naval base and strictly limiting the size of the Russian Black Sea fleet. The French reluctantly accepted this in December 1854. Peace negotiations began in Vienna in March 1855. The first two points caused no great difficulty but the discussions broke down in June on the third point. The stalemate in the Crimea was broken when Sevastopol fell to the Allies in September. Palmerston even thought of demanding that Russia should return the Crimea to Turkey, from whom she had conquered it in 1774. Napoleon toyed with the idea of making the re-establishment of an independent Poland one of their war aims, but the French people were clearly tiring of the war and nothing came of these grandiose schemes. In Russia the Tsar Nicholas I died suddenly in March 1855 and was succeeded by his son, Alexander II. At first this made little difference to either the military or diplomatic conduct of the war but Alexander was increasingly impressed by the need for fundamental reforms in his vast and inefficient empire. He was inclined to heed the warnings of the Prussian king, Frederick William IV, that the continuation of the war might lead to revolutionary outbreaks throughout Europe (5).

In November 1855 the French and the Austrians agreed, without British or Turkish participation, that the Austrians should tell the Russians that they would declare war unless the Russians agreed to two bases for peace talks: the neutralisation of the Black Sea (which would mean the exclusion of the Turkish as well as the Russian fleet) and the cession of part of Bessarabia, which belonged to Russia, to Moldavia. There was now a serious possibility that the Allies would open a second front in the Baltic, which might even threaten St Petersburg itself. Early in January 1856 the Russians agreed to a peace conference. Napoleon III was extremely anxious that it should be held in Paris, and this suggestion was acceptable to Palmerston, who favoured a tougher peace than the French were now contemplating and hoped that the combined influence of the British Foreign Secretary, Lord Clarendon, and the British Ambassador in Paris, Lord Cowley, who shared Palmerston's views, would sway Napoleon (78).

Peace was finally concluded on 30 March 1856 [doc. 52]. All the European great powers participated, including Prussia (who had taken no active part in the war) as did Turkey and Sardinia. Sardinia gained nothing material at the Conference but the position of Turkey was considerably enhanced. All the powers engaged themselves to respect the independence and the territorial integrity of the Ottoman empire.

The Sublime Porte was formally admitted 'to participate in the advantages of the public law and system (*concert*) of Europe'. The Sultan issued a *firman* (decree) recording 'his generous intentions towards the Christian population of his Empire' but it was to be clearly understood that it did not give the European powers, either singly or collectively, the right to interfere in the Sultan's relations with his subjects or with the internal administration of his empire. The Ottoman empire was thus given a more secure position among the powers of Europe and the European powers renounced any kind of protectorate over the Sultan's Christian subjects. How far Turkey could benefit from this breathing space depended on her own internal capacity for reform, which was not great, and none of the signatories of the Treaty of Paris felt compelled to spring to Turkey's defence when she again became involved in a war with Russia in 1877 (5).

Palmerston attached most significance to the neutralisation of the Black Sea. Its waters and ports were to be open to the merchant ships of all nations but they were to be closed to all warships, except a few light police vessels. No arsenals or naval dockyards were to be maintained on its coasts. The Russian Black Sea fleet ceased to exist. As Professor Anderson remarks, not until 1919 was a state again 'to be forced to submit to so obvious and flagrant a limitation of its military freedom of action' (5). Moldavia and Wallachia were given a considerable measure of autonomy, although they continued to be under the suzerainty of the Porte; Russia lost any special rights of protectorate over them. (The two Principalities were to unite in 1861 to form the state of Romania.) The rights of Serbia, another autonomous Principality within the Ottoman empire, were guaranteed by the powers collectively. Russia ceded southern Bessarabia to the Ottoman empire and was thus effectively barred from any control of the mouth of the Danube. The navigation of the Danube was to be supervised by an international commission.

Rather surprisingly, Palmerston consented to the discussion of maritime rights at Paris. Privateering was declared abolished. Except for 'contraband of war' (such as armaments), enemy goods were not to be seized in neutral ships nor neutral goods in enemy ships. Blockades should only be recognised if they were effective and not mere 'paper' blockades. Britain, in the moment of victory, thus at last conceded many of the points about which she had felt so strongly at the end of the Napoleonic wars.

The Crimean War has often been interpreted by British historians in terms of Britain's concern for the eastern Mediterranean and the defence of India and there undoubtedly was that aspect to it, but looked at from another point of view it was also essentially a European war. British, and still more French, opinion had been excited against Russia by the tribulations of Poland and, in 1849, of Hungary. The war did break the power of the 'Holy Alliance', although not quite in the way British or French radicals had foreseen. Austria's refusal to align herself with Russia in 1854—56 was resented in St Petersburg, and when the 1815 settlements were challenged in Italy in 1859 and in Germany in 1866 the old automatic coalition was no longer forthcoming. More than that, Russia, who had been one of the staunchest upholders of the sanctity of European treaties after 1815, now became, like France, a revisionist power because she wanted to change the Treaty of Paris. Russia, in fact, took advantage of the Franco-Prussian war of 1870—71 to denounce the Black Sea clauses and she regained Bessarabia in 1878 **(67, 88)**.

Asian questions loomed large in British policy in the years after 1856. The first, the quarrel with Persia, rose partly from the Crimean War. There were long-standing border and other disputes between Persia and Turkey and the Russians had assiduously cultivated Persian friend-ship, although they were not able to induce her to declare war on Tur-key as they would have liked. The cordial relations between Russia and Persia sharpened Britain's reactions when Persian forces occupied the strategic town of Herat, then under Afghan control. Britain was becom-ing very sensitive to any changes in the balance of power in Central Asia which might threaten the northern frontiers of British India. When the Persians refused to withdraw from Herat, the British sent troops from India to Bushire on the Persian Gulf and gained their point without too much difficulty, the Persians withdrew **(35)**.

The Persian campaign had weakened the British forces in India at a critical moment. The Indian Mutiny began on 8 May 1857. It was far from a national uprising. It was virtually confined to the province of Bengal but for some months the British position in India seemed to be seriously endangered. The reactions of the other European powers to Britain's difficulties were very different from those forty years later during the Boer War. Both Prussia and France offered assistance which, however, Palmerston politely declined **(78)**. The British authorities in India were fortuitously able to make up their depleted forces by de-taining British troops in transit to China and the rebellion in India was extinguished within eighteen months.

The troops in question had been going to China to take part in what became known as the *Arrow* war. Relations between Britain and China had been chequered since 1842. The Chinese were still unwilling to open what Britain regarded as normal diplomatic relations, there were still quarrels about the importation of opium, and there had been a number of violent incidents between individual Britons and Chinese which raised difficult questions of jurisdiction in view of the special privileges accorded to British residents in the treaty ports in 1842. Matters came to a head over the case of a small sailing ship, of the type known as a *lorcha*, called the *Arrow*. Because Chinese ships trading with the British were sometimes molested by their disapproving countrymen, the British authorities in Hong Kong had extended the protection of British registration, and so of the British flag, to such traders. They had not, however, exercised sufficient caution in granting such registration and Chinese smugglers, and even pirates, operated under the cover of the British flag. The Chinese authorities detained the *Arrow* and arrested her crew for piracy in October 1856. The British consul in Canton demanded that the crew he handed over to the British authorities, according to previous agreements, and that the Chinese apologise for the insult to the British flag. The Chinese reluctantly complied with the first demand but refused to apologise. The British Governor of Hong Kong, Sir John Bowring, ordered the navy to bombard Canton. The Chinese Commissioner for Canton, Yeh Mingchin, then put a price of thirty dollars on every Englishman's head. A quite savage state of war came to exist between the Chinese and the British in Canton, although neither Peking nor London was yet officially involved and life went on normally at the other treaty ports (**26, 78**).

When they heard of events in Canton the British government felt themselves to be in a dilemma. The Cabinet generally deplored Bowring's actions but the majority, led by Palmerston himself, felt that it would be impossible to appear to back down before Chinese threats. The government, however, did not have nearly such an easy time convincing Parliament in 1857 as it had had in 1840 at the time of the Opium War. Cobden moved a vote of censure in the Commons and described Bowring's actions as indefensible [**doc. 53**]. He was supported not only by William Gladstone but also by Disraeli, Lord Robert Cecil (the future Marquis of Salisbury) and Lord John Russell. Disraeli challenged Palmerston to go to the country and fight a general election on his sluggish domestic policy and his belligerent foreign policy [**doc. 53**]. Palmerston's reply was clever. He avoided the difficult questions of the *Arrow's* doubtful legal status and her almost certain criminal activities and concentrated on the threat to British civilians in China. He got a great deal of mileage out of the fact that Commissioner Yeh had acquired a reputation for brutality in the suppression of Chinese insurrections and represented him as a 'savage barbarian', whose view of the case could not reasonably be preferred to that of Bowring. Finally, he attacked Cobden directly for his lack of patriotism, as a man for whom 'everything that was English was wrong, and everything that was hostile to England was right'. It was the kind of speech which had won him the Don Pacifico debate but this time it failed; Cobden's motion was carried by 263 votes to 247. Palmerston still believed he had the country with him. The electorate would not so quickly forget his record as the man who had saved Britain during the Crimean war. He confidently asked the Queen for a dissolution of Parliament. His optimism was justified: he was returned to power with a majority of eighty-five in the House of Commons. Many of his leading opponents, including Richard Cobden himself, lost their seats.

It was all the more ironic that Palmerston was to lose office within the year on a charge of truckling to a foreign power. The extraordinary story began in January 1858 when an Italian, Felice Orsini, threw a bomb at Napoleon III as he drove in his carriage to the Paris Opera. Napoleon himself escaped unharmed but a number of bystanders were killed. Orsini was arrested and it was discovered that he had contacts in London and that, in fact, the explosive for the bomb had come from London. The French Ambassador requested Palmerston to put a stop to such activities. Nineteenth-century Britain had become a haven for political refugees as diverse as Metternich and Karl Marx; Napoleon III himself had spent some years in exile in England. The ordinary Englishman prided himself on the liberality of his laws (and the sense of security they implied), which made this hospitality possible. Responsible politicians, including Palmerston, had, however, always drawn a distinction between providing a refuge for the victims of continental upheavals and permitting the development of conspiracies. Palmerston readily consented to introduce a measure into the Commons, the Conspiracy to Murder Bill, which would tighten up the law against such activities. What he did not expect was that it would provide an opportunity for all his opponents and some of his supporters to unite against him. An amendment, seconded by John Bright, was carried against him by nineteen votes. It was a somewhat unholy alliance. Jasper Ridley sums up the event, 'The Conservatives did not have a majority in the Commons; but Bright and the pacifist Radicals, Lord John Russell and his Whigs, and Gladstone and the Peelites, were prepared to put the Conservatives in to get Palmerston out' (78). This time Palmerston did not have the country on his side; he was even booed when he went out riding. Two days later he resigned.

Palmerston himself expected to be in opposition for a long time and many other people assumed in view of his age – he was in his seventy-fourth year – that it was unlikely he would ever return to power. But the temporary coalition of interests which had overthrown him was too disparate to hold together for very long. Derby and the Conservatives had formed a government but they still did not command a majority in the Commons. Two questions made it impossible for them to continue to rely on the support of Russell and Bright and their respective supporters. The first was the domestic question of the further extension of the franchise, to which Russell and Bright were committed, but which the Conservatives at this time opposed. The second was a foreign question, the new crisis in Italian affairs.

The Italian question had entered a new phase with the Pact of Plombières between Napoleon III and Cavour in July 1858. They agreed that France should assist Piedmont in a war to expel the Austrians from Italy. Lombardy and Venetia, the Duchies of Parma and Piacenza and the Romagna should be united with Piedmont-Sardinia; in return France should receive Savoy and Nice from Sardinia. War did not break out until April 1859 when the Austrians, mistakenly assuming that they had secured their international position, issued an ultimatum that the Sardinians must disarm within three days. When the Sardinians did not do so the Austrian army crossed the River Ticino into Sardinian territory. Napoleon came to the aid of his ally. The war lasted until July 1859 when it was ended by the Armistice of Villafranca. The Austrians had been defeated in June in two major battles, Magenta and Solferino. Napoleon insisted on peace, not only because he had been genuinely sickened by the slaughter of Solferino, but also because he feared that Italian successes were outrunning his plans and that an Italian state might emerge which would be a rival rather than a client state of France. Menacing Prussian troop movements on the Rhine confirmed his determination to make peace. The Armistice of Villafranca, concluded between France and Austria without Italian participation, provided that Sardinia should have Lombardy as well as Parma and Piacenza, but not Venetia which was to remain Austrian. Modena and Tuscany were to be restored to their respective Dukes and the Romagna to the Pope. Both Austria and France would support the establishment of an Italian Confederation under the Pope **(11, 88)**.

Once again Palmerston, who returned to power just before the battle of Solferino, was faced by difficult decisions which he would have preferred to have avoided. During the British election campaign he had supported the Italian cause [**doc. 54**]. The Court favoured Austria and Palmerston still agreed with them that the preservation of

Austria as a great power was essential to the balance of power. He had come to believe, however, that Austria would be stronger without her Italian commitments than with them. The danger was that French influence would replace Austrian in Italy. The Armistice of Villafranca and Napoleon's subsequent insistence on the cession of Savoy and Nice to France, although he had carried out only part of his promises at Plombières, gave Palmerston the opportunity to condemn France and outbid Napoleon as the friend of Italian nationalism.

The sincerity of this position was soon to be tested. In April 1860 a rising took place at Palermo in Sicily. The following month Garibaldi, with the secret connivance of Cavour and Victor Emmanuel, sailed from Genoa to Sicily with his 'Thousand' Redshirts. He quickly gained control of Sicily and prepared to invade Naples. Palmerston at first suspected that there had been further secret agreements between Cavour and Napoleon III by which Napoleon would acquiesce in the Sardinian annexation of Sicily and Naples in return for the cession to France of Genoa and the island of Sardinia. He even considered giving support to the new king of Naples, Francis II, in return for promises of constitutional reforms. He was only finally convinced that there was no collusion between Napoleon and Garibaldi when the French, who feared the development of a new danger to the Papal States, which would offend the clerical party in France, themselves proposed a joint Anglo-French action to prevent Garibaldi from crossing the Straits of Messina to the mainland. Palmerston, who also feared complications in central Italy, was tempted to accept the French proposal, but he was persuaded by Lord John Russell and Gladstone to adopt a position of strict neutrality. The French chose not to intervene alone and Garibaldi was left free to conquer the whole of Italy, except Venetia and Rome itself, for Victor Emmanuel. The first Italian Parliament met in Turin in February 1861. Palmerston emerged from the events of 1859–61 with a reputation, which the facts scarcely warranted, as the friend of Italian nationalism. The reputation was built on his speeches during the election campaign of 1859; his attitude when in office had been almost entirely passive (78, 88).

While the eyes of Europe were focused on Italy, the Chinese question had flared up again. Despite their criticisms of Palmerston's actions in 1857, when the Conservatives came into office the following year they had continued to pursue the war against China with vigour. They had been joined by the French, who had their own grievances against the Chinese, notably the execution of a missionary in Shanghai. Canton was occupied in December 1857 and continued under Anglo-French control until 1860. The British and the French demanded a complete revision of all their treaties with China and Russia and the United States added similar demands in February 1858. The Chinese signed treaties with all four powers at Tientsin in June 1858. They at last agreed that foreign envoys should be allowed to come to Peking; they also promised protection for Christian missionaries, more extensive rights of travel for foreign nationals, and the opening of additional ports to foreign trade. Following the treaties, they agreed that the opium trade should be permitted on certain fairly strict conditions. Critics pointed to the irony of the powers compelling China to open her doors to the Christian religion and opium at the same time (26).

The most sensitive concession was the one allowing the opening of diplomatic relations at Peking. The British insisted that the ratifications of the new treaty should be exchanged in Peking. The Chinese refused and stopped the British and French missions forcibly at the Taku forts on the Pei-Ho River. Palmerston was now back in Downing Street and the British, like the French, reacted sharply. Reinforcements were sent and Peking itself was occupied. The campaign was marked by ugly incidents on both sides. The Chinese seized a number of European's under a flag of truce and held them as hostages in the dungeons of the Emperor's Summer Palace, where twenty of them died. As a reprisal Lord Elgin, the British Plenipotentiary, ordered that the Summer Palace be burnt. The Emperor was compelled to reaffirm the Treaties of Tientsin with some additions in the Convention of Peking of 1860. Apart from paying additional indemnities, he agreed that a British envoy should reside permanently at Peking and that he would cede Kowloon on the mainland, opposite Hong Kong (26).

Palmerston's last ministry was also marked by violent action against Japan which is much less well known than events in China. In 1863 an Englishman was killed in an affray near Yokohama. The British demanded redress and compensation and when all their terms were not met a British squadron bombarded the town of Kagoshima, causing many casualties. This too became the subject of angry exchanges in the Commons where members complained that to bomard Kagoshima was as indefensible as to bombard Bristol because a man had been killed on the road between London and Brentford (78).

Important as these Far Eastern events were they were overshadowed in most people's mind by the American Civil War, which lasted from 1861 to 1865. The war deeply divided both parliamentary and public opinion. British public opinion in general was strongly anti-slavery but it was by no means clear at the outset that the Civil War could be regarded as a crusade against slavery. On the contrary the new President, Abraham Lincoln, promised in his Inaugural address in March 1861, a month before the war broke out, that he would not interfere with the institution of slavery in the Southern States. He maintained this position until the autumn of 1862 in order to retain the support of the three slave-owning states, Maryland, Kentucky and Missouri, which did not secede with the other Southern States to form the Confederacy. Even the famous Emancipation Edict of January 1863 was hedged about with qualifications. In the early days of the war Lincoln himself insisted that the war was not about slavery but about the right of individual States to secede from the American Union [doc. 55].

British opinion was much more divided about this issue than about slavery. There were those who held that the United States had become too big and unwieldy for a single state and that division was inevitable. They pointed to the fact that all the determined secessions of recent history, whether of the Thirteen Colonies from the British empire, or of Texas from Mexico, had succeeded. Such secessions could be justified on the grounds of self-determination [doc. 56]. Moreover, several republics in North America balancing one another might be more advantageous from a European point of view than one monolithic United States. The high tariff policy of the United States was already beginning to cause concern (2).

Cotton was the most important economic factor in the situation from the British point of view. One-fifth of the whole British workforce was employed directly or indirectly in the cotton industry and eighty per cent of Britain's raw cotton came from the Southern States. It is true that grain imports from the Northern States were also important to Britain but these could if necessary be replaced from elsewhere. It was very difficult to replace the cotton supply, though by the end of the Civil War significant imports were coming from Egypt and India. The British cotton industry was cushioned from the initial impact of the war by the fact that the cotton harvest of 1860 had been a record one and had been shipped out before the war began but by 1863 the distress in Lancashire, the centre of the cotton industry, was very severe [doc. 55].

Despite this working-class opinion was remarkably solid in its support of the Northern cause. Richard Cobden and, still more, John Bright were to come out staunchly in defence of the Northern cause (2, 46). Upper-class opinion, including that of London society, was more inclined to favour the South, partly because they found it easier to identify with the 'gentlemanly' society of Virginia than with what they saw as the rough democratic pretensions of the North. The Cabinet

81

itself was divided and undecided in its policy. The Foreign Secretary, Lord John Russell, and the Chancellor of the Exchequer, William Gladstone, inclined towards the South [**doc. 56**], as did Palmerston himself. Palmerston put the matter very clearly to C.F. Adams, the United States Minister in London, an accomplished diplomat who did much to ensure British neutrality: 'We do not like slavery, but we want cotton, and we dislike very much your Morrill tariff' (2).

Early in May 1861 Britain, in proclaiming her neutrality between the two parties, implicitly recognised the Confederacy as a belligerent. The step was forced on Britain by the fact that Lincoln had proclaimed a naval blockade of the Southern States. It was thus Lincoln himself who ended the fiction that the secession was a purely domestic issue which did not concern foreign powers. Britain, in fact, aided the North by accepting the validity of the blockade even though it was often the type of 'paper blockade', which had been condemned by the Treaty of Paris of 1856. Nevertheless, Britain's recognition of the Confederacy's belligerent status, although it stopped a long way short of recognising them as an independent power, encouraged the South and irritated the North (14).

The South was very anxious to enlist European sympathy on its side and in the autumn of 1861 they sent two men, James M. Mason and John Slidell, both prominent politicians, to Europe to try to secure full recognition. Mason and Slidell evaded the North's blockade and reached Havana where they embarked on a British mail steamer, the *Trent*. Northern opinion was unduly excited about the mission and an American naval officer, Captain Wilkes, without orders from his government, intercepted the *Trent* and took Mason and Slidell off. The British government at once demanded the release of the two men and an apology. The Prince Consort, ill with typhoid fever from which he died shortly afterwards, made his last intervention in public life to persuade Lord John Russell to tone down the despatch in which the demands were made [**doc. 57**]. Public excitement grew so intense in both Britain and America that Adams's son thought that if the newly laid Atlantic cable had been in operation war could not have been avoided. As it was, tempers were allowed time to cool and the Americans conceded that Wilkes's act had been illegal and released Mason and Slidell (2).

The South failed to gain diplomatic recognition from Britain. They were rather more successful in securing armaments. The Foreign Enlistment Act of 1819 forbade the arming in British ports of ships destined for belligerents in a war in which Britain was neutral but as early as October 1861 representatives of the Southern States placed orders in Liverpool for two ships. The first, the *Florida*, ran the Northern blockade and reached Mobile, where she was armed and did considerable damage to northern shipping. Adams had protested to Russell about the building of the *Florida* but had been unable to produce firm evidence that she was meant for the Southern navy. The great controversy centred on the second ship, No. 290 as she was known in Liverpool, better known to history as the *Alabama*.

Adams complained to the British government about the ship in June and July 1862. The Foreign Office referred his complaint, as was standard practice, to the Law Officers for their opinion. Unhappily it was sent first to the Queen's Advocate on 26 July. The Foreign Office was unaware that the Queen's Advocate had had a mental breakdown and the letter did not reach the other Law Officers until the evening of 28 July. Earlier that day the ship had left the dock and anchored in the Mersey. The next day she sailed ostensibly on a trial run with guests on board. The guests were later transferred to a tug and the *Alabama* slipped away to the Azores where she was armed. She created considerable havoc among Northern shipping. The Law Officers ha⁴ finally given their opinion that the ship should be detained and the Americans protested strongly that the British could still have intercepted her if they had chosen to do so. The British government at that time refused to acknowledge responsibility or offer compensation. It was left to Gladstone's first administration to allow the question to go to arbitration and in 1872 accept the arbiters' judgment that Britain should pay the United States compensation of fifteen million dollars (2, 78).

Palmerston's government acted differently towards later ships. In April 1863 they seized another warship, the *Alexandra*, being built for the South. The firm building it subsequently took the government to court. They won their case and received damages because the government could not prove that the *Alexandra* was meant for the Southern States. After her release the *Alexandra* sailed for America but arrived too late to influence the war. Also in 1863 the South placed a contract with Laird Brothers, who had built the *Alabama*, for two ships which became known as 'Laird rams', steamers with 'piercers' or 'rams' designed to tear into the wooden hulls of the guard ships on duty outside the blockaded Southern ports. This time the British government bought the ships themselves to avoid further trouble. In the early days of the war the forces had seemed fairly evenly balanced between the North and the South, another good reason for British caution, but by the winter of 1864—65 the balance had turned decisively in favour of the North. The war ended in April 1865.

While the American Civil War was in progress the Polish question flared into renewed life. The educated classes in Poland, encouraged by Polish exiles in the West, had been stirred by the Italian example and exaggerated hopes of Alexander II's reforms to ask for the restitution of the Poland of 1772, that is before partition. The Russian reaction was repressive and in January 1861 the dissidents, many of them students, were conscripted for military service. Some escaped and began a guerrilla war but without outside assistance they had no hope of surviving for very long. French public opinion was strongly in favour of the Poles and British opinion, although less committed than the French, also sympathised with them. Russell and Palmerston both bluntly condemned the Russian action in Parliament, Palmerston insisting that it was a violation of the Treaty of Vienna. Austria and Prussia, however, both feared that the revolt might spread to their own Polish provinces and the Prussians considerably improved their relations with Russia by allowing Russian troops to enter Prussian territory to capture rebels. Palmerston refused to accept a suggestion from Napoleon III that they should protest in Berlin about this, holding that all protests should more properly be made to Russia.

In April, France, Britain and Austria all addressed separate protests to Russia but the Russians replied complaining that the rebellion had been fostered by revolutionary propaganda in the West. The three Powers tried again in June, suggesting that hostilities in Poland be suspended and that a conference of eight powers, interested in the question and signatories of the Treaty of Vienna, should meet. The Russians put forward the counter-suggestion that the matter should be settled between Russia, Prussia and Austria, the powers which had taken part in the original partition of Poland. Although the British government continued to protest vigorously, the Russians procrastinated knowing that there was little danger of Britain being able or willing to mount an armed intervention, while the Polish rebellion was steadily crushed.

In November Napoleon III put forward a new plan for a European congress but he linked it with a demand for a revision for the treaties of 1815. 'It is on the Treaty of Vienna,' he said 'that now reposes the political edifice of Europe, and yet it is crumbling away on all sides.' A new congress 'would not only regulate the fate of Poland, but would substitute for the treaties of 1815, now in decay, new stipulations apt to assure the peace of the world'. This was quite unacceptable to Britain [doc. 58]. They had no sympathy with Napoleon's revisionist views. Both Palmerston and Russell still regarded the Vienna Settlement as the basis of the European balance; indeed they had consistently criticised Russian policy in Poland because it was a breach of Vienna.

Moreover they feared that such a general reopening of questions might also lead to a revision of the Treaty of Paris and the neutralisation of the Black Sea. The Poles were not aided, although the expressions of sympathy from the West may well have encouraged them to prolong a hopeless fight. The French were alienated by the decisive tones in which Russell had rejected Napoleon's November proposals (13, 78).

The estrangement of Britain and France over Poland had its effect on the next European crisis, that concerning the Duchies of Schleswig and Holstein. In March 1863 the king of Denmark, Frederick VII, published a Patent which, while it recognised the special status of Holstein as a member of the German Confederation, declared that Schleswig was an integral part of the Danish state. This was quite unacceptable to the Diet of the German Confederation who threatened military intervention. Although the British government advised Frederick to withdraw the Patent, which was not strictly compatible with the Treaty of London of 1852, both Russell and Palmerston spoke sharply against German intervention. Russell declared that Great Britain 'could not see with indifference a military occupation of Holstein, which is only to cease upon terms injuriously affecting the constitution of the whole Danish Monarchy'. Palmerston in a famous speech in the Commons of 23 July 1863 told his hearers that the independence, the integrity, and the rights of Denmark' must be maintained and he was convinced

> if any violent attempt were made to overthrow those rights and inter-
> fere with that independence, those who made the attempt would
> find in the result that it would not be Denmark alone with which
> they would have to contend [doc. 59] .

Gladstone was to recall later that the speech made no great sensation in the House or in Britain at the time, although it was quickly seized upon in Denmark.

On 13 November 1863 the Danish Parliament voted a new constitution ratifying the Patent of 30 March. Two days later Frederick VII died. On hearing the news, Queen Victoria remarked, truly if callously, that 'this wretched King' could have chosen no more unfortunate moment to die. In accordance with the Treaty of London he was succeeded by Christian of Glucksburg, whose daughter, Alexandra, had earlier in the year married the Prince of Wales. But Frederick the son of Duke Christian of Augustenburg, now came forward to assert his claims to the Duchies, arguing that he was not bound by his father's renunciation. Liberal opinion in Germany supported him. So did Victoria, who remembered that the Prince Consort had always held that Augustenburg had been unjustly deprived of his rights (78).

Frederick, however, lacked the support of one key figure, Otto von Bismarck, who had been Prime Minister of Prussia since September 1862. Bismarck hoped to secure the Duchies for Prussia. The real prize at stake was the important port of Kiel. Bismarck was able to win Austrian support because the Austrians did not want to ally themselves with the German liberals and felt that to accept the right of Schleswig and Holstein to secede from Denmark might afford a precedent for Venetia. On 24 December 1863 Saxon and Hanoverian troops, acting on behalf of the German Confederation, occupied Holstein and proclaimed Frederick of Augustenburg the rightful Duke of Schleswig and Holstein, and on 14 January 1864 the German Diet formally denounced the arrangements of 1852, to which they had never been a party. Bismarck, at the cost initially of considerable unpopularity in Prussia, dissociated himself from this. On 16 January 1864 Prussia and Austria, independently of the Diet, demanded, as signatories of the Treaty of London, that Denmark should enforce that treaty and withdraw the new constitution. When the Danes did not comply, an Austro-Prussian army entered the Duchies on 1 February (13).

The Danes looked to Britain for assistance, relying mainly on Russell and Palmerston's recent speeches. Russell was still warlike. He suggested joint intervention with France, by which Britain should send a fleet to Copenhagen and France mobilise her forces on the Rhine. The idea did not appeal to Palmerston. He still saw France as a greater threat to European peace and British interests than Prussia [doc. 60]. Napoleon, he thought, would be only too glad to seize the opportunity of undoing the Treaty of Vienna and acquiring Rhenish Prussia. In any case, Napoleon had no intention of cooperating with Britain in a war over Schleswig-Holstein. He was still smarting from Russell's rejection of his proposals for a Congress on Poland and had already committed himself to his Mexican adventure, the ill-fated attempt to put the Archduke Maximilian on the Mexican throne. Instead he made overtures to Berlin, suggesting that France would acquiesce in Prussia acquiring the Duchies in return for 'compensation' for France in the Rhineland.

The Danes were encouraged when Britain intervened to deter an Austrian squadron from entering the Baltic. Public opinion in Britain was certainly strongly on their side. The legal intricacies of the conflict counted for little against the belief that 'little' Denmark was being bullied by sabre-rattling Prussia. The popularity of the new Princess of Wales helped to confirm this feeling. A conference of representatives of the interested powers, including the German Confederation, did in fact meet in London in April and an armistice was arranged on 12 May. The Danes, still believing that in the last resort the British would help them, and objecting to negotiations while the Duchies remained occupied, refused to make concessions. When the armistice expired on 16 June it was not renewed. The day before the British Cabinet had met: a proposal to send a fleet to help to defend Copenhagen was carried by Palmerston's casting vote but Palmerston himself conceded that it was impossible to act with such a divided Cabinet (78).

A few days later, Palmerston made a very feeble defence of his policy in the Commons, still hinting that if the Austrians and the Prussians continued their advance to Copenhagen and threatened Denmark's existence as an independent state, Britain might yet act. He no longer carried conviction. The House laughed. Disraeli, who had made a very effective speech indicting every aspect of Palmerston's policy, only just failed to carry his Vote of Censure expressing 'regret that while the course pursued by Her Majesty's Government had failed to maintain their avowed policy of upholding the integrity and independence of Denmark it has lowered the just influence of this country in the capitals of Europe, and thereby diminished the securities of peace'. Palmerston's government survived only by relying on the votes of the Cobdenites who, although themselves bitterly critical of Palmerston's actions, announced that they would vote for him because it would be a vote for peace. Jasper Ridley comments, 'Bright and Cobden hailed it as a great victory. After fighting for years against Palmerston's foreign policy, they had won at last – under the leadership of Palmerston' (78).

One may wonder how much Palmerston's policy had changed. He had always been blunt, sometimes threatening, in speech but cautious in action. In earlier crises, such as those of 1848–49 he had gained a great reputation by standing on the touchlines and doing very little. He had good reason for being cautious in 1864. Britain could not fight without a continental ally and it is doubtful whether France or Russia would have joined her, however tactful Palmerston had been. Across the Atlantic the American Civil War was still being waged and it was never impossible that Britain might have been drawn into that. Certainly he should have been cautious in his speeches too, but he had some grounds for maintaining (although no one listened to him in an excited House of Commons in June 1864) that he had never, even in his speech of 23 July 1863, spoken of unilateral English intervention but of a reaction by the Powers of Europe. Palmerston had always carried much by bluff: this time his bluff had been called – by Bismarck.

It is often suggested that Palmerston was much less successful in his last ministry in the 1860s than he had been in the 1830s because

Part Three: Assessment

6 British Foreign Secretaries

It is all too easy to take advantage of hindsight and see British foreign policy between the Napoleonic wars and 1865 in the light of the developments of the next fifty years, the unification of Germany, the Bismarckian alliance system, the outbreak of the First World War and the massive social changes which that engendered and which resulted in the transfer of political power to entirely new groups and classes. This is the easier because so many studies of the subject were written during the great classical period of the study of diplomatic history between the two world wars, when men's minds were dominated by a desire to know what had caused the First World War and, if possible, to avoid such mistakes in future. This approach is reinforced by the fact that studies of the nineteenth century traditionally begin in 1815. The Vienna Settlement is taken as the starting point and the changes in it are then chronicled, often with the implication that the forces which succeeded, such as nationalism, were the (desirable) forces of the future and that a statesman's policy can be judged by the extent to which he recognised and aided such forces. Such an approach is not altogether invalid, and it may even contain important lessons for futurologists who seek to predict the future by an assessment of the present, but the danger is that it wrenches British foreign policy in the first half of the nineteenth century out of its context.

British policy was really forged in the fires of the revolutionary and Napoleonic wars. What all British statesmen from Pitt onwards sought was stability in Europe (57, 72). The Vienna settlement [doc. 15] approximated closely enough to British views of what the peace settlement should be [docs. 10, 11] for them to see it as a satisfactory arrangement which should be defended so long as its defence did not, in other ways, upset the stability and balance of Europe. They had no doctrinaire attachment to legitimacy as (with some reservations) the eastern powers had. But, equally, they had no doctrinaire attachment to constitutional states, except in so far as they believed that (apart from being a flattering imitation of the British system) constitutional states tended to be peaceful, stable states, with influential middle classes who made good trading partners.

This preference for constitutional states did not extend to republics. Most men would have agreed with Palmerston that republics had an unfortunate tendency to pursue aggressive foreign policies (p. 60). This stability was to be achieved by the maintenance of the equilibrium of Europe and the guiding principle which Castlereagh, Canning and Palmerston shared above all others [doc. 6] was that of the balance of power. Some of Palmerston's criticisms of Aberdeen arose from the fact that he thought that Aberdeen did not understand this principle and consequently did not appreciate how serious it was to lower British influence in countries like Greece or Spain. Occasionally British statesmen thought of it as an ideological balance, such as that between the Quadruple Alliance and the Holy Alliance, but usually they did not. Any kind of permanent ideological alignment was precluded by the fact that all British statesmen thought it essential to maintain the heterogeneous Austrian empire as a Great Power in Central Europe [doc. 45].

William Pitt had laid down in some detail the settlement he wished to see at the end of the Napoleonic wars, as well as projects for maintaining it [docs. 1, 10]. Of the four men who most influenced British foreign policy in the first half of the nineteenth century three, Canning, Castlereagh and Aberdeen, regarded themselves as the direct disciples and heirs of Pitt, and the fourth, Palmerston, always declared himself to be the pupil of Canning. But Pitt's legacy was a confused one, and each man drew on different parts of it. Dr Derry suggests that Castlereagh represented the 'administrative' legacy of Pitt (28). He preferred to work quietly at the conference table and had little taste, and less talent, for explaining his aims and methods to Parliament, let alone to a wider public. This, combined with circumstances unconnected with foreign affairs, his Irish policy and his association with the government's repressive measures after 1815, meant that he was not understood and his policy was not appreciated by contemporaries or by the early historians of the period. He was contrasted, to his disadvantage, with Canning who was supposed to represent liberalism, nationalism and English patriotism. Academic battle was joined in the 1920s and 1930s by Professor Temperley who championed Canning and Professor Webster who defended Castlereagh (91, 98, 99). In the end a consensus was reached that the two men differed surprisingly little in their policies or their assessment of British interests. Canning probably had a hand in Castlereagh's most famous political testament, the State Paper of May 1820 [doc. 19] and he used Castlereagh's draft instructions for the British delegate at the Congress of Verona in 1822.

Too much has been made of Canning's comment in a letter to a friend, Charles Bagot, also in 1822, 'For *Europe*, I shall be desirous now and then to read *England*' and Castlereagh has too often been called 'a good European', or at least the phrase has been misunderstood. Castlereagh had not preferred the interests of Europe to those of England. He had believed that usually what benefited Europe also benefited England, but where this was clearly not the case, as over maritime rights, no one had spoken more decisively than Castlereagh [doc. 12]. Pitt had not clearly recognised the importance of emergent nationalism in Europe (80), but Castlereagh as well as Canning had done so. He wrote to Lord Cathcart in September 1813,

> The present Confederacy ... is distinguished from former Confederacies ... by the national character which the war has assumed throughout the respective states. On former occasions it was a contest of sovereigns, in some instances perhaps, against the prevailing sentiment of their subjects; it is now a struggle dictated by the feelings of the people of all ranks as well as by the necessity of the case [cf. docs. 7, 8].

No man who had lived through 1798 in Ireland could doubt either the power or the potential dangers of national passions (28).

The real contrast between Castlereagh and Canning was in personality and the public image they presented. Canning, unlike the formal and expressionless Castlereagh (9), was witty, brilliant (his enemies said flashy) and a good public speaker in the rhetorical tradition of the times. He had a strong sense of humour and poked fun at his own maiden speech in a journal he kept at the time. 'I know no pleasure', he wrote, '(*sensual* pleasure I had almost said) equal to that which I experienced', but he knew he had gestured too wildly. Lord Camden beside him got 'a plaguey hard blow on the shoulder' while 'Pitt who was beneath me *sidled* a little out of the way and Dundas was obliged to *bob* to save his *wig* from confusion'. But he soon mastered the medium. In 1826 he employed verbal legerdemain in a famous speech to compel the Commons to concentrate on the independence of the former Spanish colonies and to cover up the fact that he had entirely failed to prevent France's successful intervention in mainland Spain. 'I looked another way,' said Canning, 'I sought materials of compensation in another hemisphere. Contemplating Spain, such as our ancestors had known her, I resolved that if France had Spain, it should not be Spain "with the Indies". I called the New World into existence to redress the balance of the Old' (45).

Ironically, it was the attitude of European conservatives which established Canning's reputation as a crusader for liberalism and nationalism. Metternich called Canning's death 'an immense event, for the man was a whole revolution in himself'. This idea was taken up by British admirers such as Sir James Mackintosh, who wrote: 'His death was an event in the internal history of every country. From Lima to Athens every nation struggling for independence or existence was filled by it with sorrow and dismay' (45). In fact, Canning was well aware of the limits of both British interests and of British power when it came to fostering liberalism or nationalism. 'Let us not,' he once said 'in the foolish spirit of romance, suppose that we alone can regenerate Europe' (91). Harold Nicolson concludes that Canning was 'not, as Metternich supposed, a Jacobin in disguise; he was a philosophical Tory of the school of Burke' (68).

Much the same thing was to happen to Palmerston. He became the *bête noire* of European conservatives during the revolutions of 1848–49 and this was reinforced by his supposed championship of Italian nationalism in 1859–60. Palmerston, the lifelong opponent of parliamentary reform at home, found himself, to his own surprise, the hero of the radicals. Like Canning he had a considerable gift for rhetoric and repartee and he played up to his image, not only in Parliament but also in the country, notably during the election contests at Tiverton, the seat he held for thirty years (78, cf. [doc. 54]). Palmerston believed that bluff was an essential part of diplomacy and perhaps he bluffed his countrymen as well as foreigners into believing that his successes were greater than they were. His achievements in Europe were really very modest and some of them were the result of well calculated inaction. He could not aid Poland or Hungary; his influence on Italian unification was marginal; his plans for the Iberian peninsula were only partly successful – he could not prevent the Spanish marriages; in Schleswig-Holstein, where he had achieved a real success in 1852, he spectacularly backed the wrong horse in 1863. Only in Belgium was a solution found that was completely in line with Palmerston's plans. Palmerston took a more decisive stand on the Eastern Question than he did on many European issues and here his influence on the course of events was undeniable. Contemporaries, however, wondered whether the solution that was found to the Mehemet Ali problem in 1840 was worth the quarrel with France. Not only contemporaries but also historians have long debated whether the check which was undoubtedly given to Russian power in 1856 (88) justified the miseries of the Crimean War. Aberdeen was more successful than Palmerston in coming to terms with the United States.

Despite Aberdeen's protestations in the Lords in 1852 (p. 66), there were real differences between his policy and that of Palmerston. Palmerston cultivated the image of the blustering Englishman much more than Canning had done, even in small things like his notorious unpunctuality and his, sometimes studied, discourtesy in keeping foreign diplomats waiting (78). Perhaps, as has been suggested, it was but one manifestation of the often aggressive nationalism which seized almost all European peoples in the nineteenth century. The British people loved it and Palmerston played to his audience, publishing documents more freely than any of his predecessors, even Canning, had done, and himself writing in the newspapers. The contrast between Palmerston and Aberdeen was to some extent the same as that between Canning and Castlereagh. Aberdeen, like Castlereagh, could not project himself in public. He had an unfortunate manner of public speaking, which seemed to his opponents like sneering (36). But the difference went deeper than that: Aberdeen had a genuinely internationalist outlook. He could always see the point of view of France or the United States and feel compelled to make allowances for it. It was an attitude of mind which led Palmerston to accuse him, sometimes justifiably, of weakness. But it was also a view of international affairs which he passed on to Gladstone – who greatly admired him – who developed it into a new vision of international morality.

Some of Palmerston's successes outside Europe, such as the 'opening up' of China, are not ones which the twentieth century tends to look back at with any pride. They illustrate, however, just as Canning's more acceptable policy in South America does, the high priority which British Foreign Secretaries gave in the nineteenth century to the defence of British trading interests. The Foreign Office may often have been ignorant of the technicalities of trading needs and conditions – it certainly totally lacked all the specialised agencies which a modern Foreign Office takes for granted – but it entirely accepted that for Britain trade was a vital interest, in the literal nineteenth-century definition of that phrase, as being necessary to a nation's survival.

None of the four men most concerned with the formulation of British foreign policy in this period was himself a merchant or had the kind of firsthand knowledge of trade that, say, Cobden had. But neither in fact were they representative of the long-established aristocrat class which is usually assumed to have dominated diplomacy in early nineteenth-century Europe. Canning was the son of an impecunious Irish barrister, who had had to make his own way in the world and had known real poverty as a child. Castlereagh was the child of an Ulster commercial family. Palmerston, although an English landowner, had only an Irish title and his family had previously only been on the fringes of political power in England. Aberdeen had a rather better claim to be a true patrician but his was a Scots title and his family too had not previously been prominent in English politics. Even Wellington was the younger son of a not very prominent Irish family, who won his high honours on the battlefield.

A.J.P. Taylor reminds us that when we speak of 'the British' in the context of foreign policy we often mean 'the few members of the Foreign Office who happened to concern themselves with this question' (89). Those who dissented from official policy are often as interesting as those who formulated it. There were no clear party political divisions in approaches to foreign policy in early nineteenth-century England. Castlereagh, Canning and Aberdeen called themselves Tories or Conservatives. Palmerston, at least in the period when he determined foreign policy, called himself a Whig and later a Liberal. But this does not truly represent their differences. Much in Aberdeen's policy would have been acceptable to the Liberals in the late nineteenth century, much in Palmerston's was appropriated by the Conservatives from Disraeli onwards. Sometimes 'dissent' in foreign policy was represented by the odd eccentric like David Urquhart but reaction to Palmerston's policies brought into existence one important school of thinking on British foreign policy, the Manchester School, its hard rationalism represented by Richard Cobden, its more emotional appeal by John Bright [docs. 5, 51, 53] Gladstone himself was later to call it 'a noble error' (89), with its perhaps ultimately unrealistic belief that nationalistic foreign policy could be replaced by international harmony, but it runs like a counter-motif through British foreign policy in the middle of the nineteenth century.

Part Four: Documents

1 The Concepts of Foreign Policy

THE CONCERT OF EUROPE
The Concert of Europe, in the sense of an arrangement between the Great Powers to maintain the peace, had a tentative beginning in the discussions for the Third Coalition against Napoleon in 1805.

document 1

William Pitt's views

... the first Step must be, to fix as precisely as possible, the distinct objects to which such a Concert is to be directed.

These ... appear to be three:

1st To rescue from the Dominion of France those countries which it has subjugated since the beginning of the Revolution, and to reduce France within its former limits, as they stood before that time.

2ndly To make such an arrangement with respect to the territories recovered from France, as may provide for their Security and Happiness, and may at the same time constitute a more effectual barrier in future against Encroachments on the part of France.

3rdly To form, at the Restoration of Peace, a general Agreement and Guarantee for the mutual protection and Security of different Powers, and for re-establishing a general System of Public Law in Europe.

Pitt to the Russian Ambassador in London, 19 January 1805, *Parliamentary Papers*, xiii (1814–15) 261; quoted in (93) p.11.

document 2

The Treaty of Chaumont, 1 March 1814

At this time the distinction between an arrangement to guarantee 'a general System of Public Law in Europe' and a fighting coalition against Napoleon was a fine one. As the end of the Napoleonic wars approached the coalition against France and against any renewal of French aggression became more restricted and specific. Pitt was now dead and the need to combat the 'universalist' ideas of the French Revolution

Documents

(which had played a part in the 1805 discussions) was less pressing. Article V of the Treaty of Chaumont simply read:

Article V The High Contracting Parties [*Austria, Britain, Prussia and Russia*], reserving to themselves to concert together, on the conclusion of a Peace with France as to the means best adapted to guarantee to Europe, and to themselves reciprocally, the continuance of the Peace, have also determined to enter without delay, into defensive engagements for the Protection of their respective States in Europe against every attempt which France might make to infringe the order of things resulting from such a Pacification.

E. Hertslet, *The Map of Europe by Treaty*, Butterworths, 1875, iii, 2045.

document 3

The Treaty of Quadruple Alliance, 20 November 1815

What is usually regarded as the Congress System proper was set up by a treaty signed by the four allies at the same time as the Second Treaty of Paris.

Article VI To facilitate and to secure the execution of the present Treaty, and to consolidate the connections which at the present moment so closely unite the four Sovereigns for the happiness of the World, the High Contracting Parties have agreed to renew their meetings at fixed periods, either under the immediate auspices of the Sovereigns themselves, or by their respective Ministers, for the purpose of consulting upon their common interests, and for the consideration of the measures which at each of these periods shall be considered the most salutary for the repose and prosperity of Nations, and for the maintenance of the Peace of Europe.

The Treaty of Alliance and Friendship between Great Britain, Austria, Prussia and Russia, signed at Paris, 20 November 1815; in E. Hertslet, *The Map of Europe by Treaty*, i, 375.

document 4

The Holy Alliance, 26 September 1815

The Tsar Alexander had not, however, abandoned his more mystical concept of the bonds between nations and on 18 September 1815 he

96

had persuaded Austria and Prussia to sign the document that became known as the Holy Alliance.

Article I Conformable to the words of the Holy Scriptures, which command all men to consider each other as brethren, the Three contracting Monarchs will remain united by the bonds of a true and indissoluble fraternity, and considering each other as fellow countrymen, they will, on all occasions and in all places, lend each other aid and assistance; and, regarding themselves towards their subjects and armies as fathers of families, they will lead them, in the same spirit of fraternity with which they are animated, to protect Religion, Peace, and Justice.

E. Hertslet, *The Map of Europe by Treaty*, i, 318.

THE BALANCE OF POWER
document 5

Richard Cobden's challenge

The argument about 'the balance of power' continued through the whole period. Some, like Richard Cobden, thought it a dynastic concept rendered obsolete by the rise of new democratic forces.

Why do we trouble ourselves with these continental politics? . . . Our general excuse is – and it is a phrase that is stereotyped in the despatches of the noble Lord the Foreign Secretary [*Lord Palmerston*] – that we have a policy founded on what is called 'the balance of power' – a thing I never could understand; but I believe the present balance is a figment that was supposed to have grown out of what is termed the great settlement of Vienna, but which I term the great unsettlement of Vienna. But can we, in the face of those growing popular interests, any longer base our foreign policy on that Treaty of Vienna?

Hansard, 3rd ser., clxxvi, 838 (5 July 1864).

document 6

Palmerston's reaffirmation

. . . it is a doctrine founded on the nature of man. It means that it is to the interest of the community of nations that no one nation should acquire such a preponderance as to endanger the security of the rest; and it is for the advantage of all that the smaller Powers should be respected in their independence and not swallowed up by their more powerful neighbours. That is the doctrine of the balance of power, and it is a doctrine worthy of being acted upon.

Hansard, 3rd ser., clxxvi, 1280 (8 July 1864)

THE IDEOLOGICAL FORCES

(a) The new forces of nationalism and liberalism

document 7

Canning's recognition of Spanish nationalism

When the bold spirit of Spain burst forth indignant against the oppression of Buonaparte [*in 1808*] I discharged the glorious duty ... of recognising without delay the rights of the Spanish nation, and of at once adopting that gallant people into the closest amity with England.

Hansard, 2nd ser., viii, 1509 (30 April 1823).

document 8

Palmerston on the forces which overthrew Napoleon

When Bonaparte was to be dethroned, the Sovereigns of Europe called up their people to their aid; they invoked them in the sacred names of Freedom and National Independence: the cry went forth throughout Europe: and those, whom Subsidies had no power to buy, and Conscription no force to compel, roused by the magic sound of Constitutional Rights, started spontaneously into arms. The long-suffering Nations of Europe rose up as one man, and by an effort tremendous and wide spreading, like a great convulsion of nature, they hurled the conqueror from his throne. But promises made in days of distress, were forgotten in the hour of triumph.

Hansard, 2nd ser., xxiii, 82 (10 March 1830).

(b) The forces of resurgent conservatism

document 9

Edmund Burke on the dangers of revolution

The violence of the French Revolution led some to reject the ideas of the Enlightenment and to seek for stability in the old certainties.

They [*the original leaders of the French Revolution*] have found their punishment in their success. Laws overturned; tribunals subverted; industry without vigour; commerce expiring; the revenue unpaid, yet the people impoverished; a church pillaged, and a state not relieved; civil and military anarchy made the constitution of the kingdom; everything human and divine sacrificed to the idol of public credit, and national bankruptcy the consequence; and, to crown all, the paper securities of impoverished fraud, and beggared rapine, held out as currency for the support of the empire, in lieu of the two great recognized species that represent the lasting, conventional credit of mankind, which disappeared and hid themselves in the earth from whence they came, when the principle of property, whose creatures and representatives they are, was systematically subverted.

Reflections on the Revolution in France; Burke's Political Writings, Nelson, pp. 242–3.

2 The Age of Canning and Castlereagh

BRITISH WAR AIMS

document 10

William Pitt's aims

William Pitt formulated these in 1805. (They should be read in conjunction with document 1.)

Should it be possible to unite in Concert with Great Britain and Russia, the two other great Military Powers of the Continent, there seems little doubt that such an union of Force would enable them to accomplish all that is proposed. – But if . . . it should be found impossible to engage Prussia in the Confederacy, it may be doubted whether such Operations could be carried on in all the Quarters of Europe as would be necessary for the success of the whole of this Project. The chief points however to which . . . this doubt is applicable relate to the question of the entire Recovery of the Netherlands and the Countries occupied by France on the left Bank of the Rhine. – His Majesty considers it essential, even on this Supposition to include nothing less than the Evacuation of the North of Germany and Italy, the Re-establishment of the Independence of the United Provinces, and of Switzerland, the Restoration of the Dominions of the King of Sardinia, and the Security of Naples; But, on the side of the Netherlands, it might perhaps be more prudent in this case to confine the views of the Allies, to obtaining some moderate acquisition for the United Provinces, calculated ... to form an additional Barrier for that Country.

Pitt to the Russian Ambassador in London, 19 January 1805; quoted in (93) pp. 11–12. (Some of this section was omitted in *Parl. Papers*, xiii (1814–15) 261.)

Castlereagh's aims

document 11

Castlereagh formulated these aims more precisely in 1813 although he was still well aware that the final settlement would depend on the military situation. He proposed that the following secret articles should be attached to a treaty of alliance.

1. The re-establishment of Austria in the degree of power and extent of territory which she possessed previous to 1805, as well in Italy as in Germany.
2. The reconstruction of the Prussian Monarchy in the same extent of population and territory in which it existed previous to 1806.
3. The dissolution of the Confederation of the Rhine – Germany to be rendered independent, and the provinces thereof in the north, either united to France or subjected to the family of Napoleon, to be restored.
4. The Duchy of Warsaw to cease to exist, as at present, and its future to be regulated without the intervention of France.
5. The separation, with an adequate barrier, of Holland from France.
6. The re-establishment of the ancient and lawful dynasty of Spain.
7. The liberation of Italy from the rule and influence of France.
8. The restoration of the House of Brunswick-Luneburgh (both Electoral and Ducal) to their dominions and rights.
9. The exclusion of French power and influence from the northern side of the Baltic by the annexation of Norway to the Crown of Sweden.
10. The restoration of the Kingdom of Naples or a suitable equivalent to His Sicilian Majesty.

Castlereagh to Lord Cathcart, 18 September 1813; quoted in (97), pp. 26–7.

document 12

Castlereagh on Britain's 'maritime rights'

I cannot omit again impressing upon your Lordship the importance of awakening the Emperor's [*of Russia*] mind to the necessity, for his own interests as well as ours, of peremptorily excluding from the negotiations every maritime question. If he does not, he will risk a similar misunderstanding between those Powers on whose union the safety of Europe now rests. Great Britain may be driven out of a Congress, but not out of her maritime rights, and, if the Continental Powers knew their own interests, they will not hazard this.

Castlereagh to Lord Cathcart, 14 July 1813; quoted in **(97)** p. 14.

document 13

Prussia's role

The containment of France leads to the accretion of Prussian power.

I am always led to revert with considerable favour to a policy which Mr. Pitt, in the year 1806, had strongly at heart, which was to tempt Prussia to put herself forward on the left bank of the Rhine, more in military contact with France. I know there may be objections to this, as placing a power peculiarly military, and consequently somewhat encroaching, so extensively in contact with Holland and the Low Countries. But, as this is only a secondary danger, we should not sacrifice it to our first object, which is to provide effectually against the systematic views of France to possess herself of the Low Countries and the territories on the left bank of the Rhine – a plan which, however discountenanced by the present French Government, will infallibly revive, whenever circumstances favour its execution.

Castlereagh to Wellington, 1 October 1814, *Memoirs and Correspondence of Viscount Castlereagh*, x, 144–5.

document 14

British views on Poland

The Polish question proved particularly difficult.

However this question of Poland may now end, it cannot be settled either creditably or satisfactorily . . .

Memorandum

. . . It is obvious that an arrangement may be made with respect to the Duchy of Warsaw upon either of the following three principles:

1st It may be divided between the three great Powers, and so made to constitute a part of each of their dominions. Or

2ndly It may be preserved as an independent State under an independent prince. Or

3rdly It may be assigned to one of the three great Powers as an independent State, which under the present circumstances would be Russia.

Of these three alternatives, I should certainly consider the third the worst for the general interests of Europe . . .

I cannot, however, conceal from you that this last project would be less unpopular in this country than the measure of complete partition, and consequently of Polish annihilation. If we are to come to either of these alternatives, I think it would be very desirable that there should, if possible, be some record of our having expressed our opinion how desirable it would be to restore Poland on the principle of 1792, and of our having made some effort for that which we are more entitled to ask, the independence of the Duchy of Warsaw under a neutral Sovereign.

Liverpool to Castlereagh, 14 October 1814; quoted in **(97)**, pp.210–11.

THE TREATY OF VIENNA

document 15

The terms of the Treaty, 9 June 1815

Article I The Duchy of Warsaw . . . is united to the Russian Empire. It shall be irrevocably attached to it by its Constitution, and be possessed by His Majesty the Emperor of all the Russias, his heirs and successors in perpetuity. . . . The Poles, who are respective subjects of Russia, Austria, and Prussia, shall obtain a Representation and National Institutions, regulated according to the degree of political consideration, that each of the Governments to which they shall belong shall judge expedient and proper to grant them.

Article LIII The Sovereign Princes and Free Towns of Germany, under which denomination, for the present purpose, are comprehended their Majesties the Emperor of Austria, the Kings of Prussia, of Denmark, and of the Netherlands; that is to say:

The Emperor of Austria and the King of Prussia, for all their possessions which anciently belonged to the German Empire;

The King of Denmark, for the Duchy of Holstein;

And the King of the Netherlands, for the Grand Duchy of Luxemburg; among themselves a perpetual Confederation, which shall be called 'The Germanic Confederation'.

Article LXV The ancient United Provinces of the Netherlands and the late Belgic Provinces . . . shall form . . . the Kingdom of the Netherlands, . . . The title and the prerogatives of the Royal dignity are recognised by all the Powers in the House of Orange-Nassau.

Article LXXXIV The Declaration of the 20th March [*the guarantee, on the part of all the Powers, of the perpetual Neutrality of Switzerland, in her new frontiers*] is confirmed in the whole of its tenor.

Article LXXXVI The States which constituted the former republic of Genoa, are united in perpetuity to those of his Majesty the King of Sardinia . . .

Article XCIII . . . the Powers . . . recognise His Majesty the Emperor of Austria . . . as legitimate Sovereign of the following Provinces and Territories; Istria, Dalmatia, the ancient Venetian Isles of the Adriatic . . . the City of Venice, with its waters, as well as all the other provinces and districts of the formerly Venetian States . . . the Duchies of Milan and Mantua . . .

Article CIII The Marches . . . are restored to the Holy See. The Holy See shall resume possession of the Legations of Ravenna, Bologna and Ferrara . . .

[*The Emperor of Austria*] shall have the right of placing Garrisons at Ferrara and Commachio.

E. Herstlet, *The Map of Europe by Treaty*, i, 216, 243, 248, 259, 260, 262–3, 267–8.

document 16
A nineteenth-century view of the Vienna Settlement

We believe that all the disturbances which have agitated Europe from 1815 to the present time, all the discontents and revolutions of these thirty-two years, and all the moral inquietude which more or less agitates society have been caused by the unnatural and forced partition of Europe by the Congress of Vienna. Its measures for the establishment of peace and tranquillity in Europe have proved the germs of all wars and revolutions which have since occurred, because the only interests there cared for were those of dynasties, families and privileged classes, without any consideration of national feeling, or of the inevitable wants of that new state of society which the Revolution had created.

Marquis Massimo d'Azeglio in 1847, quoted *Hansard*, 3rd ser., clxxvi, 839.

document 17
A twentieth-century view of the Vienna Settlement

When he wrote the following passage Sir (as he later became) Charles Webster was a British army officer seconded to help with the preparations for the Paris Peace Conference of 1919.

The work of the Congress of Vienna was dealt with faithfully by the publicists of its own time, and has been severely handled by historians in the century that followed. The spectacle of a dozen statesmen transferring 'souls' by the 100,000 from one sovereign to another has inspired many mordant pens; and in the light of the history of the nineteenth century the validity of these criticisms cannot be disputed. Such criticisms, however, neglect the fact that the Congress was the close of one epoch as well as the beginning of another. The main object of the statesmen of the day was to overthrow the Napoleonic Empire completely; and in that object they succeeded to a much greater degree than they expected. . . . Had any attempt been made to substitute for the contracts, written and unwritten, which had united Europe against Napoleon, the vague principles of nationality and democracy, so imperfectly understood alike by the peoples and the statesmen, the result would have been disastrous. The primary need of Europe, once the Napoleonic tyranny was overthrown, was a period of peace; and this the statesmen at Vienna undoubtedly secured in a far greater degree than the most sanguine of the publicists of the time dared to hope.

C.K. Webster, **(96)** pp. 164–5.

THE CONGRESS SYSTEM

Castlereagh's view of its purpose diverges from that of the Eastern Powers.

document 18

The Troppau Protocol

It is instructive to compare this with Mr Brezhnev's declaration justifying the Russian intervention in Czechoslovakia in 1968, 'When forces hostile to Socialism try to turn a nation toward the restoration of capitalism, this becomes more than the nation's affair, but a matter of concern for all Socialist countries', 'The Observer', 17 November 1968.

(1) States, forming part of the European Alliance, which have undergone a change, due to revolution, in the form of their constitution and the results of which menace other States, *ipso facto* cease to be part of the Alliance and remain excluded from it, until their situation gives guarantees of legal order and stability. (2) The Allied Powers do not limit themselves to announcing this exclusion; but faithful to the principles which they have proclaimed and to the respect due to the authority of every legitimate government as to every act emanating from its own free will, agree to refuse recognition to changes brought about by illegal methods. (3) When States where such changes have been made, cause by their proximity other countries to fear immediate danger, and when the Allied Powers can exercise effective and beneficial action towards them, they will employ, in order to bring them back to the bosom of the Alliance, first friendly representation, secondly measures of coercion, if the employment of such coercion is indispensable.

Quoted in **(98)**, p. 295.

document 19

Castlereagh's State Paper of 5 May 1820

Although mainly directed to the question of the insurrection in Spain this contained Castlereagh's considered opinion of the undesirability of intervention in the internal affairs of other states even in the case of revolution.

There can be no doubt of the general Danger which menaces more or less the stability of all existing Governments from the Principles which are afloat, and from the circumstances that so many States of Europe are now employed in the difficult task of casting anew their Governments upon the Representative Principle; but the notion of revising, limiting or regulating the course of such Experiments, either by foreign Council or by foreign force, would be as dangerous to avow as it would be impossible to execute, and the Illusion too prevalent on this Subject, should not be encouraged in our Intercourse with the Allies ...

In this Alliance as in all other human Arrangements, nothing is more likely to impair or even destroy its real utility, than any attempt to push its duties and obligations beyond the Sphere which its original Conception and understood Principles will warrant: – It was an union for the Reconquest and liberation of a great proportion of the Continent of Europe from the Military Dominion of France, and having subdued the Conqueror it took the State of Possession as established by the Peace under the Protection of the Alliance; – It never was however intended as an Union for the Government of the World, or for the Superintendence of the Internal Affairs of other States ...

It provided specifically against an infraction on the part of France of the State of Possession then created; It provided against the Return of the Usurper or any of his family to the Throne: it further designated the Revolutionary Power which had convulsed France and desolated Europe, as an object of its constant solicitude; but it was the Revolutionary Power more particularly in its Military Character actual and existent within France against which it intended to take Precautions, rather than against the Democratic Principles, then as now, but too generally spread throughout Europe ...

[*The Tsar of Russia does not have to take account of public opinion but*] The King of Great Britain, from the nature of our Constitution, has on the contrary all His means to acquire through Parliament, and he must well know that if embarked in a War, which the Voice of the Country does not support, the efforts of the strongest Administration which ever served the Crown would soon be unequal to the prosecution of the Contest ...

In this country at all times, but especially at the present conjuncture, when the whole Energy of the State is required to unite all reasonable men in defence of our existing Institutions, and to put down the spirit of Treason and Disaffection which in certain of the Manufacturing Districts in particular, pervades the lower orders, it is of the greatest moment, that the publick Sentiment should not be distracted or divided, by any unnecessary Interference of the Government in events passing abroad, over which they can have none or at best very imperfect means of controul ...

... We shall be found in our place when actual danger menaces the System of Europe, but this Country cannot, and will not, act upon abstract and speculative Principles of Precaution: – The Alliance which exists had no such purpose in view in its original formation: – It was never so explained to Parliament; if it had, most assuredly the sanction of Parliament would never have been given to it, and it would now be a breach of Faith were the Ministers of the Crown to acquiesce in a Construction being put upon it, or were they to suffer themselves to be betrayed into a Course of Measures, inconsistent with those Principles which they avowed at the time, and which they have since uniformly maintained both at Home and Abroad.

Quoted in **(93)** pp. 48–63. (This document was published in part by Canning, *Parl. Papers*, xix (1823), pp. 69–71.)

THE AFFAIRS OF SOUTH AMERICA

document 20

The Polignac Memorandum October 1823

Canning was determined that the European Powers should not reconquer the Spanish colonies which had made good their independence. He obtained a promise to this effect from the Prince de Polignac, the French Ambassador in London, and made it public.

That the near approach of a crisis, in which the Affairs of Spanish America must naturally occupy a great share of the attention of both Powers [*Britain and France*], made it desirable that there should be no misunderstanding between them on any part of a subject so important.

That the British Government were of opinion, that any attempt to bring Spanish America again under its ancient submission to Spain, must be utterly hopeless; . . .

That the British Government would . . . remain strictly neutral in a War between Spain and the Colonies . . . but that the junction of any foreign Power in an enterprise of Spain against the Colonies would be viewed by them as constituting an entirely new question; and one upon which they must take such decisions as the interest of Great Britain might require.

The Prince de Polignac declared, that his Government believed it to be utterly hopeless to reduce Spanish America to the state of its former relation to Spain; – that France disclaimed, on Her part, any intention or desire to avail Herself of the present state of the Colonies, or of the present Situation of France towards Spain, to appropriate to Herself any part of the Spanish Possessions in America; or to obtain for Herself any exclusive advantages. . . . Lastly, that She abjured, in any case, any design of acting against the Colonies by force of Arms.

Quoted in **(93)** pp. 70–76; published in part *Parl. Papers*, xxiv (1824), pp. 641–53.

THE GREEK WAR OF INDEPENDENCE

document 21

Russian policy towards the Ottoman Empire

Russian policy was not so bent on the destruction of the Ottoman empire as the British supposed but the likelihood of its collapse presented European diplomacy with one of its stiffest tests.

The Committee unanimously recognized:

That the advantages of maintaining the Ottoman Empire in Europe are greater than the difficulties which it presents.

That its fall would henceforth be contrary to the true interests of Russia.

Report of the Special Committee on the Affairs of Turkey, 16 September 1829; printed in **(6)**, p. 36.

document 22

The Protocol of St Petersburg, 4 April 1826

Britain, at the Greek request, had offered her mediation to the Turks. Canning seized the opportunity both to tie Russia's hands by reaching an agreement with her and of by-passing any Congress.

I. That the Arrangement to be proposed to the Porte, if that Government should accept the proffered Mediation, should have for its object, to place the Greeks towards the Ottoman Porte, in the relation hereafter mentioned:

Greece should be a Dependency of that Empire, and the Greeks should pay to the Porte an annual Tribute, the amount of which should be fixed by common consent. They should be exclusively governed by authorities to be chosen and named by themselves, but in the nomination of which authorities the Porte should have a certain influence.

In this state, the Greeks should enjoy a complete liberty of Conscience, entire freedom of Commerce, and should, exclusively, conduct their own internal Government.

Hertslet, i, 741–2.

document 23

The Protocol of Poros, 12 December 1828

After Canning's death Greece achieved complete independence but within very restricted borders. The Protocol of Poros foreshadows the final settlement of 1830 and explains the principles on which it was made.

I. The only parts of Greece actually freed from the presence of the Turks ... are, the Morea, the Islands, and some detached portions of Roumelia.
II. Those parts of the Greek continent which have taken the most active and persevering share in the Insurrection, and in which the Christian population generally, in consequence of its numbers, and of the comparative extent of its possessions, has the best claims to ... Independence ... are to be found between the Isthmus of Corinth, and the high mountains which traverse the Continent from the Gulf of Arta to the Gulfs of Zeitoun and Volo.

Hertslet, ii, 798–9. (Terms agreed by Britain, Russia and France.)

document 24

Convention of London, 7 May 1832

This was an agreement between Britain, France, Russia and Bavaria.

The Courts of Great Britain, France and Russia, exercising the power conveyed to them by the Greek nation, . . . have resolved to offer the Crown of the new Greek State to the Prince Frederick Otho of Bavaria, second son of His Majesty the King of Bavaria . . .

Article IV Greece under the Sovereignty of Prince Otho of Bavaria, and under the Guarantee of the 3 Courts, shall form a monarchical and independent State . . .

Hertslet, ii 893–5.

3 Lord Palmerston as Foreign Secretary

document 25

Bases destined to establish the separation of Belgium from Holland, 27 January 1831

Palmerston's handling of the Belgian crisis is generally taken to show him at the peak of his powers.

Fundamental Arrangements

Article I The limits of Holland shall comprise all the territories, fortresses, towns and places which belonged to the ancient Republic of the United Provinces of the Netherlands in the year 1790.

Article II Belgium shall consist of all the remainder of the territories which received the denomination of the Kingdom of the Netherlands in the Treaties of the year 1815, except the Grand Duchy of Luxemburg, which being possessed by the Princes of the House of Nassau under a different title, forms, and shall continue to form, part of the Germanick Confederation.

Article VI Belgium, within those limits . . . shall form a perpetually neutral State. The five Powers guarantee to it that perpetual neutrality, as well as the integrity and inviolability of its territory within the above-mentioned limits.

Article VIII The port of Antwerp . . . shall continue to be solely a port of commerce.

Parliamentary Papers, xlii (1833), 304—5.

document 26

Palmerston's attitude to constitutional states

Henry Lytton Bulwer complained in the Commons that Austria and Prussia were contravening the independence accorded to the separate states of Germany by the Treaty of Vienna, by coercing them into anti-revolutionary activities. Palmerston declined to intervene on the grounds that the Treaty of Vienna had not been breached but declared his concern for constitutional states.

. . . I am prepared to admit, that the independence of constitutional States, whether they are powerful, like France or the United States, or of less relative political importance, such as the minor states of Germany, never can be a matter of indifference to the British Parliament, or, I should hope to the British public. Constitutional States I consider to be the natural Allies of this country; and whoever may be in office conducting the affairs of Great Britain, I am persuaded that no English Ministry will perform its duty if it be inattentive to the interests of such States.

Hansard, 2nd ser., xiv, 1045 (2 August 1832).

THE IBERIAN PENINSULA
Palmerston consistently supported constitutional, as against absolutist, parties in Spain and Portugal.

document 27

The 'Quadruple Alliance', 22 April 1834

(a) The Treaty

Article I His Imperial Majesty the Duke of Braganza, Regent of the Kingdom of Portugal and the Algarves in the name of the Queen Donna

Maria the Second, engages to use all the means in his power to compel the Infant Don Carlos to withdraw from the Portuguese Dominions.

Article II Her Majesty the Queen Regent of Spain during the minority of her daughter Donna Isabella the Second, Queen of Spain . . . engages to cause such a body of Spanish Troops as may hereafter be agreed upon between the two Parties, to enter the Portuguese territory, in order to co-operate with the troops of Her Most Faithful Majesty, for the purpose of compelling the Infants Don Carlos of Spain and Dom Miguel of Portugal to withdraw from the Portuguese Domions . . .

Article III His Majesty the King of the United Kingdom of Great Britain and Ireland engages to co-operate, by the employment of a Naval Force. . .

Additional Articles, 18 August 1834.

Article I His Majesty the King of the French engages to take such measures in those parts of his Dominions which adjoin to Spain, as shall be best calculated to prevent any Succours of men, arms, or warlike stores, from being sent from the French Territory to the Insurgents in Spain.

Hertslet, ii, 942–3, 949–50.

(b) Palmerston's Comments

I reckon this to be a great stroke. In the first place, it will settle Portugal, and go some way to settle Spain also. But, what is of more permanent and extensive importance, it establishes a quadruple alliance among the constitutional states of the west, which will serve as a powerful counterpoise to the Holy Alliance of the east.

Palmerston to his brother, William Temple, 21 April 1834; quoted in **(21)**, ii, 180.

THE EASTERN QUESTION

document 28

The Treaty of Unkiar Skelessi, 8 July 1833

This Russo-Turkish Treaty was a serious set-back for British policy in the Near East. It was mistakenly believed in London that the Treaty gave Russian warships free passage through the Dardanelles in time of war.

Article 1 There shall be for ever peace, amity and alliance between His Majesty the Emperor of all the Russias and His Majesty the Emperor of the Ottomans, their empires and their subjects, as well by land as by sea. This alliance having solely for its object the common defence of their dominions against all attack, their Majesties engage to come to an unreserved understanding with each other upon all the matters which concern their respective tranquillity and safety, and to afford to each other mutually for this purpose substantial aid, and the most efficacious assistance.

Article 3 . . . His Majesty the Emperor of all the Russias, in the event of circumstances occurring which should again determine the Sublime Porte to call for the naval and military assistance of Russia . . . engages to furnish, by land and by sea, as many troops and forces as the two high contracting parties may deem necessary . . .

Separate and Secret Article . . . Nevertheless, as his Majesty the Emperor of all the Russias, wishing to spare the Sublime Ottoman Porte the expense and inconvenience which might be occasioned to it, by affording substantial aid, will not ask for that aid if circumstances should place the Sublime Porte under the obligation of furnishing it [*instead the Sublime Porte*] shall confine its action in favour of the Imperial Court of Russia to closing the strait of the Dardanelles, that is to say, to not allowing any foreign vessels of war to enter therein under any pretext whatsoever.

Hertslet, ii 925–8.

document 29
Palmerston's desire to co-operate with France in the Eastern Question

The Cabinet yesterday agreed that it would not do to let Mehemet Ali declare himself independent, and separate Egypt and Syria from the Turkish Empire. They see that the consequences of such a declaration on his part must be either immediately or at no distant time conflict between him and the Sultan. That in such a conflict the Turkish troops would probably be defeated; that then the Russians would fly to the aid of the Sultan, and a Russian garrison would occupy Constantinople and the Dardanelles; and once in possession of those points, the Russians would never quit them. We are, therefore, prepared to give naval aid to the Sultan against Mehemet, if necessary and demanded; and we intend to order our Mediterranean fleet immediately to Alexandria, in order to give Mehemet an outward and visible sign of our inward resolve. We should like the French squadron to go there too at the same time, if the French are willing to do so.

Palmerston to Lord Granville (British Ambassador in Paris), 8 June 1838; quoted, (21), ii, 267.

document 30
Convention for the Pacification of the Levant, 15 July 1840

Palmerston failed to carry France with him in his Eastern policy and came to an agreement with Russia, Prussia and Austria to which France was not a party.

Article I His Highness the Sultan having come to an agreement with their Majesties [*of Great Britain, Austria, Prussia and Russia as to the arrangement to be offered to Mehemet Ali*], their Majesties engage to act in perfect accord, and to unite their efforts in order to determine Mehemet Ali to conform to that arrangement. . . .

Article II If the Pasha of Egypt should refuse to accept the above-mentioned arrangement . . . their Majesties engage to take, at the request of the Sultan, measures concerted and settled between them, in order to carry that arrangement into effect.

Article IV . . . but it is agreed, that such measures shall not derogate in any degree from the ancient rule of the Ottoman Empire, in virtue of which it has in all times been prohibited for Ships of War of Foreign Powers to enter the Straits of the Dardanelles and of the Bosphorus . . .

Separate Act
1. His Highness promises to grant to Mehemet Ali, for himself and for his descendants in the direct line, the administration of the Pashalic of Egypt; and His Highness promises, moreover, to grant to Mehemet Ali, for his life, with the title of Pasha of Acre, and with the command of the Fortress of St John of Acre, the administration of the southern part of Syria . . . [*If Mehemet Ali did not accept this within a specified time limit, the offer would be modified or withdrawn.*]

Hertslet, ii, 1008–15.

document 31
Convention respecting the Straits of the Dardanelles and of the Bosphorus, 13 July 1841

France joined the other Powers to conclude a new treaty about the Straits the following year.

Article I His Highness the Sultan, on the one part, declares that he is firmly resolved to maintain for the future the principle invariably established as the ancient rule of his Empire, and in virtue of which it has at all times been prohibited for the Ships of War of Foreign Powers to enter the Straits of the Dardanelles and of the Bosphorus; and that, so long as the Porte is at Peace, His Highness will admit no Foreign Ship of War into the said Straits.

And their Majesties [*of Great Britain, Austria, France, Prussia and Russia*], on the other part, engage to respect this determination of the Sultan, and to conform themselves to the principle above declared.

Hertslet, ii, 1024–6.

document 32
Whig divisions

Palmerston's policy on the Eastern Question split the Cabinet and led to intrigues between Francophile Whigs and French ministers which verged on unconstitutional, or even treasonable, practice.

Did ever country present such a spectacle in its administration? Their differences and cabals are become notorious as the secrets of the town-crier; one-third is with Palmerston, one-third, it seems, against him, and one-third do not know which way to go. The 'Bear' Ellice [*Edward Ellice, a radical M.P. and an old opponent of Palmerston*], they say, (and it must have been a pure love of intrigue and mischief), urged Thiers [*the French Prime Minister*] to resist the policy of Palmerston, assuring him that the Cabinet would never meet any *real* French resistace. . . . Lord Holland [*Chancellor of the Duchy of Lancaster*] writes to Guizot [*the French Ambassador in London*], and tells him everything. Clarendon [*Holland's successor as Chancellor of the Duchy of Lancaster*] talks to everybody, follows in the tail of Charles Greville [*Clerk of the Privy Council*] and throws confusion into the Cabinet, which, said Lord Minto [*First Lord of the Admiralty*] was very unanimous and reciprocal in confidence, till Clarendon joined it. The Duc de

Broglie [*a former French premier*] writes to Lord Lansdowne [*Lord President of the Council*], and Lord Lansdowne writes to Broglie; can this be done without communication, on my Lord's part, of his misgivings, waverings, etc. etc., and all the mischievous puerilities of the English Cabinet? ... The fact is there has been foul intrigue to replace Palmerston ... Meanwhile, Melbourne, the Prime Minister, suffers all this, having neither authority not principle!

Lord Shaftesbury's Journal, 12 November 1840; quoted in E. Hodder, *Life of the Seventh Earl of Shaftesbury*, Cassell, 1887, vol. 1, p.317.

THE OPIUM WAR

document 33

Gladstone's Speech in the Commons, 7 April 1840

Palmerston carried the majority of British opinion with him in his action against China but he was severely criticised by the young William Gladstone.

The Chinese government had acted in accordance with their fixed determination, to try to put a stop to opium smuggling. Had they not a strict moral right to put a stop to it? Was it not mere mockery to affect – to pretend indignation as to the pernicious consequences of the opium trade, and yet exhaust all the armory of ingenuity and eloquence to prove that the Chinese were not justified in taking effectual means of crushing that trade ... [*The British flag*] has always been associated with the cause of justice, the opposition to oppression, with respect for national rights, with honourable commercial enterprize, but now, under the auspices of the noble Lord, that flag is hoisted to protect an infamous contraband trade...

Hansard, 3rd ser., vol liii, 811, 816.

THE SLAVE TRADE

document 34

Palmerston's speech in 1841

Palmerston detested the Trade and made strenuous efforts to stamp it out. His greatest parliamentary speech against it was on 16 July 1844 but he here explains what practical steps he had taken.

When we came into office in 1830, we found the slave-trade carried on to an immense extent, and under various flags, notwithstanding the treaties we had the concluded with Spain, Portugal, Brazil, the Netherlands, and Sweden; and notwithstanding the declaration made at the Congress of Vienna. . . . But we were told, and by many of the most zealous friends of abolition, that our treaties would be of no avail to suppress the slave-trade until every maritime state in Christendom should have joined in the league to put it down; for as fast as we drove the trade from one flag it would take shelter under another . . . We have laboured hard, and I am proud to say not without some success. At the present moment we have treaties concluded and ratified with France, Spain, Portugal, the Netherlands, Sweden, Denmark, the Hans [*sic*] Towns, Sardinia, Tuscany and Naples; we have been negotiating a treaty between England, France, Austria, Russia, and Prussia. . . . Nor have we been idle as to America. We have concluded treaties which have been ratified, with Brazil, Buenos Ayres, Venezuela, and Haiti. [*Others are in prospect*] if we succeed in these various negotiations . . . we shall have enlisted in this league against the slave-trade every state in Christendom which has a flag that sails on the ocean, with the single exception of the United States of North America; and I cannot believe, that the American people, descended from the same ancestors as ourselves, imbibing from their earliest infancy the same principles of liberty, and the same doctrines of religion, will long stand aloof. . .

Hansard, 3rd ser., lviii, 649—51 (18 May 1841)

4 Palmerston and Aberdeen: Two Rival Schools?

ABERDEEN'S APPROACH TO FOREIGN POLICY
Aberdeen had a deep hatred of war, based on his experiences of the closing phase of the Napoleonic wars. He was never converted to the doctrine that to avoid war one should prepare for it.

document 35

Aberdeen on Leipzig after the battle

How shall I describe the entrance to this town? For three or four miles the ground is covered with bodies of men and horses — many not dead, wretches wounded, unable to crawl, crying for water, amidst heaps of putrefying bodies. Their screams are heard at an immense distance, and still ring in my ears. The living, as well as the dead, are stript by the barbarous peasantry, who have not sufficient charity even to put the miserable wretches out of their pain. I will not attempt to say more of this. Our victory is most complete. It must be owned that a victory is a fine thing, but one should be at a distance to appreciate it.

Aberdeen to his sister-in-law, Lady Maria Hamilton, 22 October 1813, British Museum, Add. MSS. 43325.

document 36
Aberdeen and Peel disagree on military preparedness.

(a) Aberdeen

I am glad to perceive that Guizot [*the French Prime Minister*] agrees with me in the opinion which I have long entertained, and have frequently expressed, that the old maxim of 'preparing for war in order to preserve peace' is entirely inapplicable to the condition of Great Powers, and to the political system of modern times and present state of society.

Aberdeen to Peel, 11 October 1845, British Museum, Add. MSS. 40455.

(b) Peel

[*Guizot*] may be perfectly sincere as an individual in controverting the maxim, *Bellum para, pacem habebis*. But, as the Minister of France . . . can he point to her practice as confirming his theory? Was the expenditure of some 20 millions on the fortifications of Paris a confirmation of it? . . . Has France an army of 350,000 men? Has she a National Guard of one million of men? Has she made great and successful exertions to improve her marine and increase her naval strength? . . . I am a strenuous advocate for peace, – for peace with France especially . . . but when I see the weakness of civil authority in France, the fruitful germs of war with France which will spring up in the event – the probable event of war with the United States; when I look back on the suddenness with which there have been within our short memory revolutions in the Government of France, and forward to events which *may* occur on the death of Louis Philippe, I cannot feel sanguine as to the future . . .

Peel to Aberdeen, 17 October 1845, British Museum, Add. MSS. 43065.

RELATIONS WITH AMERICA

document 37

The Maine Boundary Dispute

(a) The question at issue as defined in 1833

It appears to me that the time is arrived when, notwithstanding the insuperable constitutional Difficulties in the way of the Government of the United States [*a reference to States' Rights*], the question of boundary must be settled by a mutual concession of pretensions, and by a fair and equitable division of the disputed territory between the two Claimants. If the position of that territory is examined, an adjustment of the interests of both Parties does not seem to present any difficulty. The intrinsic value of the soil is unknown beyond the timber which covers it. The essential interests of the two Governments consist in its position — in its locality. Great Britain must contend for a secure and uninterrupted communication by the usual and accustomed Road between Halifax and Quebec. It must be the interest of the United States to procure as large an extension of Territory as possible on the frontier of Maine.

Sir Charles Vaughan (the British Minister in Washington) to Palmerston, 4 July 1833, copy in 'Memorandum on North Eastern Boundary', Aberdeen Papers, British Museum, Add. MSS. 43123.

(b) Aberdeen's indifference to the details of the settlement.

... for myself, I must declare that if we shall at last be driven to quarrel with the United States, I sincerely pray that we may take our Stand on some great principle of National policy, or of humanity and justice, and that we not go to war for a few miles, more or less, of a miserable pine swamp.

Aberdeen to Ashburton, 3 March 1842, Add. MSS. 43123.

document 38

The Slave Trade and Maritime Rights

The British wanted the Americans to accord them the 'Right of Search', or at least the 'Right of Visit' (to check a ship's nationality), to help the British West Africa squadron operate efficiently against suspected slavers. The Americans refused because of their resentment against old British practices such as impressment.

(a) Aberdeen to the American Minister in London

It can scarcely be maintained that Great Britain should be bound to permit her own subjects, with British vessels, and British capital, to carry on before the eyes of British officers, this detestable traffick in human beings . . . merely because they had the audacity to commit an additional offence by fraudulently usurping the American flag.

Aberdeen to Andrew Stevenson (American Minister in London), 13 October 1841, Public Record Office, F.O. 84/376.

(b) Ashburton on impressment

Ashburton wished the British government to renounce the right of impressment.

Impressment, as a system, is an anomaly hardly bearable by our own people. To the foreigner it is undeniable tyranny, which can only be imposed upon him by force and submitted to by him so long as that force continue. [*America is now much stronger than in 1812*] . . . can Impressment ever be repeated? I apprehend nobody in England thinks it can. Here there can be no doubt that the first exercise of this practice would produce War. Is it not then better to surrender with a good grace a pretended right, while the surrender may bring you some credit, than to maintain what you will have no power to execute?

Ashburton to Aberdeen, no 7, 12 May 1842, P.R.O. F.O. 5/379.

Aberdeen refused on the grounds that it would be 'tantamount to an absolute and entire renunciation of the indefeasible right inherent in the British Crown to command the allegiance of its subjects, wherever found', Aberdeen to Ashburton, no 9, 3 June 1842, F.O. 5/378.)

RELATIONS WITH FRANCE

A rapprochement with France was traditionally Whig, not Tory, policy but Aberdeen, and more reluctantly Peel, maintained very close relations, 1841–6.

document 39

Peel on the value of an understanding with France

It is for the interest of England, for the interest of France, for the interest of Europe, and for the interest of civilisation that a good understanding should be maintained between England and France. A bad understanding may prevail between distant countries and may not lead to war: but between England and France you have hardly an alternative between a cordial and friendly understanding and hostility.

Hansard, 3rd ser lxxvii, 89 (4 February 1845).

But relations were strained in many parts of the world.

document 40

Public excitement over Tahiti

Long ere this can be received the public will be in possession of the underhand and ungentlemanly manner in which Admiral Dupetit Thouars forced the Protectorate on Queen Pomare.... The paper presented to the Queen was worded in such a Jesuitical manner as to deceive Europe into the belief that it was a voluntary act of the Queen; whereas the alternative was the French guns opening on her people and laying her towns in ashes . . .

Mr Pritchard was for many years a missionary out here. For ten years he has served his country as British Consul; he is beloved by the Queen, respected and looked up to by the people.... The French have placed themselves in a sad degraded state when they thus war against those, all the world over respected by belligerents, – the clergy and the women . . . where has England suffered an outrage equal to that which was put on her last evening? . . . A British subject, and he our consul and the representative of the Majesty of England, treated as a common convict, seized in the open day, in the presence of his family, hurried like a vile malefactor along the streets, jeered at by French soldiers as he was dragged in front of the barracks. Is England thus low that she will not call down for vengeance on the dastards' heads who thus dare to insult the person to whose keeping she had confided her honour?

'A British Officer', writing from Tahiti, *The Times*, 30 July 1845.

document 41

The Spanish Marriage Question

(a) *Queen Victoria, accompanied by the Earl of Aberdeen, visited the French royal family at the Chateau d'Eu in September 1845. An apparently amicable agreement was reached.*

I think the marriage of the Queen of Spain is the subject on which the greatest interest is felt at this moment. . . . Both the King and Guizot said they had no objection to the Duke of Seville and that if it should be found that Count Trapani was impossible, they would willingly support him. [*Seville and Trapani were both Bourbons and the French did not wish the Queen to marry out of the House of Bourbon.*]

With respect to the Infanta, they both declared in the most positive and explicit manner, that until the Queen was married and had children, they should consider the Infanta precisely as her sister, and that any marriage with the French Prince would be entirely out of the question.

Aberdeen to Sir Robert Peel, 8 September 1845, in *Letters of Queen Victoria*, Murray, 1908, ii, 44—5.

(b) *Palmerston, on returning to office, sent the British Ambassador in Madrid a list of candidates, headed by a non-Bourbon, Prince Leopold of Saxe-Coburg.*

The choice of a husband for the Queen of an independent country is obviously a matter with which the Governments of other countries are not entitled to interfere, unless there should be a probability that the choice would fall upon some Prince so directly belonging to the reigning family of some powerful foreign State, that he would be likely to connect the policy of the country of his adoption with the policy of the country of his birth, in a manner that would be injurious to the balance of power, and dangerous to the interests of other States. But there is no person of this description among those who are now named as candidates for the hand of the Queen of Spain; those candidates being reduced to three, namely, the Prince Leopold of Saxe-Coburg, and the two sons of Don Francisco de Paula [*the Dukes of Seville and Cadiz*] .

Palmerston to Henry Bulwer, 19 July 1846, *Parliamentary Papers* lxix (1847) p. 280.

THE REVOLUTIONS OF 1848

document 42

The principles of Palmerston's foreign policy

(a) Speech to Parliament.

I hold with respect to alliances, that England is a Power sufficiently strong, sufficiently powerful, to steer her own course, and not to tie herself as an unnecessary appendage to the policy of any other Government. I hold that the real policy of England – apart from questions which involve her own particular interests, political or commercial – is to be the champion of justice and right, pursuing that course with moderation and prudence. [*If she does so*] she will never find herself altogether alone. She is sure to find some other State of sufficient power, influence and weight, to support and aid her ... Therefore I say that it is narrow policy to suppose that this country or that is marked out as the eternal ally or the perpetual enemy of England. We have no eternal allies, and we have no perpetual enemies. Our interests are eternal and perpetual, and those interests it is our duty to follow. ... And if I might be allowed to express in one sentence the principle which I think ought to guide an English Minister, I would adopt the expression of Canning, and say that with every British Minister, the interests of England ought to be the shibboleth of his policy.

Hansard, 3rd ser., xcvii, 122–3 (1 March 1848).

(b) Report to Queen Victoria

Although events of the greatest importance have been passing in rapid succession in almost every part of Europe, the position of your Majesty's Government has been one rather of observation than of action, it being desirable that England should keep herself as free as possible from unnecessary engagements and entanglements ...

Palmerston to Queen Victoria, 18 April 1848, in *The Letters of Queen Victoria*, Murray, 1908, ii, 171.

document 43

The revolution in France

What extraordinary and marvellous events you give me an account of. It is like the five acts of a play, and has not taken up much more time.

Strange that a king who owed his crown to a revolution brought about by royal blindness and obstinacy should have lost it by exactly the same means, and he a man who had gone through all the vicissitudes of human existence, from the condition of a schoolmaster to the pomp of a throne. . . . Continue at your post. . . . Our principles of action are to acknowledge whatever rule may be established with apparent prospect of permanency, but none other. We desire friendship and extended commercial intercourse with France, and peace between France and the rest of Europe. We will engage to prevent the rest of Europe from meddling with France, which indeed we are quite sure they have no intention of doing. The French rulers must engage to prevent France from assailing any part of the rest of Europe. Upon such a basis our relations with France may be placed on a footing more friendly than they have been or were likely to be with Louis Philippe and Guizot.

Palmerston to Lord Normanby, the British Ambassador in Paris, 26 February 1848; quoted in (7) i, 76–8.

document 44

The revolutions in Italy

I cannot regret the expulsion of the Austrians from Italy. I do not believe, Sire, that it will diminish the real strength nor impair the real security of Austria as a European Power. Her rule was hateful to the Italians, and has long been maintained only by an expenditure of money and an exertion of military effort which left Austria less able to maintain her interests elsewhere . . . I should wish to see the whole of Northern Italy, united into one kingdom, comprehending Piedmont, Genoa, Lombardy, Venice, Parma and Modena; and Bologna would, in that case, sooner or later unite itself either to that state or to Tuscany. Such an arrangement of Northern Italy would be most conducive to the peace of Europe, by interposing between France and Austria a neutral state strong enough to make itself respected, and sympathising in its habits and character neither with France nor with Austria. . . .

Palmerston to King Leopold of the Belgians, 15 June 1848; quoted in (7) i, 98.

document 45

The revolution in Hungary

Austria is a most important element in the balance of European power. Austria stands in the centre of Europe, a barrier against encroachment on the one side, and against invasion on the other. The political independence and liberties of Europe are bound up, in my opinion, with the maintenance and integrity of Austria as a great European Power. . . . The House will not expect me to follow those who have spoken today by endeavouring to pass judgement either way between the Austrian Government and the Hungarian nation . . . even the success of Austria, if it is simply a success of force, will inflict a deep wound on the fabric and frame of the Austrian empire . . . it is devoutly to be wished that this great contest may be brought to a termination by some amicable arrangement between the contending parties, which shall on the one hand satisfy the national feelings of the Hungarians, and on the other hand not leave to Austria another and a larger Poland within her empire. Britain should let her opinion be known. Opinions, if they are founded in truth and justice, will in the end prevail against the bayonets of infantry, the fire of artillery, and the charge of cavalry.

Palmerston on the entry of Russian forces into Hungary, 21 July 1849; *Hansard*, 3rd ser., cvii, 809–13.

document 46

The Don Pacifico Affair

(a) Palmerston's defence of his actions

I therefore fearlessly challenge the verdict which this House, as representing a political, a commercial, a constitutional country, is to give on the question now brought before it, whether the principles on which the foreign policy of Her Majesty's Government has been conducted, and the sense of duty which has led us to think ourselves bound to afford protection to our fellow subjects abroad, are proper and fitting guides for those who are charged with the Government of England; and whether, as the Roman, in days of old, held himself free from indignity, when he could say *Civis Romanus sum*; so also a British subject, in whatever land he may be, shall feel confident that the watchful eye and strong arm of England will protect him against injustice and wrong.

Hansard, 3rd ser., cxii, 444 (25 June 1850).

(b) Gladstone's rebuke

What then, Sir, was a Roman citizen? He was the member of a privileged caste: he belonged to a conquering race, to a nation that held all others bound down by the strong arm of power. For him there was to be an exceptional system of law; for him principles were to be asserted, and by him rights were to be enjoyed, that were denied to the rest of the world. Is such, then, the view of the noble Lord, as to the relation that is to subsist between England and other countries?

Ibid., 586 (27 June 1850).

document 47

The quarrel with the Queen

The Queen remonstrates

With reference to the conversation about Lord Palmerston which the Queen had with Lord John Russell the other day, and Lord Palmerston's disavowal that he ever intended any disrespect to her by the various neglects of which she has so long and so often to complain, she thinks it right, in order to prevent any mistake for the future, shortly to explain what it is she expects from her Foreign Secretary. She requires: (1) That he will distinctly state what he proposes to do in a given case, in order that the Queen may know as distinctly to what she has given her Royal sanction; (2) Having once given her sanction to a measure, that it be not arbitrarily altered or modified by the Minister; such an act she must consider as failing in sincerity towards the Crown, and justly to be visited by the exercise of her Constitutional right of dismissing that Minister. She expects to be kept informed of what passes between him and the Foreign Ministers before important decisions are taken, based upon that intercourse; to receive the Foreign Despatches in good time, and to have the drafts for her approval sent to her in sufficient time to make herself acquainted with their contents before they must be sent off. The Queen thinks it best that Lord John Russell should show this letter to Lord Palmerston.

Queen Victoria to Lord John Russell, 12 August 1850, *The Letters of Queen Victoria*, Murray, 1908, ii, 264.

THE EASTERN QUESTION

document 48

The Nesselrode Memorandum, 3 December 1844

*This was a contingency agreement between Britain and Russia to con-
cert their policy if, contrary to their hopes, the Ottoman Empire collapsed but, published at the beginning of the Crimean War, it reinforced
suspicions that the Tsar wanted a partition.*

... The object for which Russia and England will have to come to an
understanding may be expressed in the following manner:
1. To seek to maintain the existence of the Ottoman Empire in its
present state, so long as that political combination shall be possible.
2. If we foresee that it must crumble to pieces, to enter into previous
concert as to everything relating to the establishment of a new order
of things, intended to replace that which now exists, and in conjunction with each other to see that the change which may have occurred
in the internal situation of that Empire shall not injuriously affect either
the security of their own States and the rights which the Treaties assure
to them respectively, or the maintenance of the balance of power in
Europe.

Parliamentary Papers, lxxi (1854) 868.

document 49

The Seymour Conversations

The Tsar's remarks to the British Ambassador also alarmed London

[*The Tsar said*] Now Turkey ... has by degrees fallen into such a state
of decrepitude that ... eager as we all are for the continued existence
of the man (and that I am as desirous as you can be for the continuance
of his life, I beg you to believe), he may suddenly die upon our hands;
we cannot resuscitate what is dead; if the Turkish Empire falls, it falls
to rise no more; and I put it to you, therefore, whether it is not better
to be provided beforehand for a contingency, than to incur the chaos,
confusion, and the certainty of an European war, all of which must
attend the catastrophe if it should occur unexpectedly, and before
some ulterior system has been sketched; this is the point to which I
am desirous that you should call the attention of your Government.

... it could happen that circumstances put me in the position of occupying Constantinople, if nothing has been foreseen, if we must leave everything to chance ...

Sir G. Hamilton Seymour to Lord John Russell, 22 January 1853, *Parliamentary Papers*, lxxi (1854), 837—8.

document 50

Popular enthusiasm for the Crimean War

The Poet Laureate, Lord Tennyson, summed up the feeling that the war was a crusade.

... so I wake to the higher aims
Of a land that has lost for a little her lust of gold,
And love of a peace that was full of wrongs and shames,
Horrible, hateful, monstrous, not to be told;
And hail once more to the banner of battle unroll'd! ...
For the peace, that I deem'd no peace, is over and done,
And now by the side of the Black and the Baltic deep,
And deathful-grinning mouths of the fortress, flames
The blood-red blossom of war with a heart of fire.

Lines from 'Maud', *Poems of Tennyson*, Oxford University Press, 1917, p. 466.

document 51

Richard Cobden on the futility of war

We are at the end of the second year's campaign; the Allies have lost in killed and wounded, nearly as many men as it cost Napoleon, in actual combat, to gain possession of Moscow, and still Sebastopol is not wholly in our power.... Let us assume the most favourable result ... that, after a series of obstinate and bloody encounters, the Russians are compelled to retreat, and leave the whole of the Crimea in the hands of our Allies. Will the Allied powers keep possession of the Crimea? If so, an army will be required to occupy it. Or, is it to be abandoned? If so, in twelve hours the Cossack lances will be seen above the ruins of Sebastopol; and then what was the motive for taking it at so great a cost?

From 'What next — and next?' (January 1856), *The Political Writings of Richard Cobden*, Wm. Ridgway, 1878, i, 259—61, 299.

5 Lord Palmerston as Prime Minister

document 52

The Eastern Question

The Treaty of Paris, 30 March 1856

Article VII Her majesty the Queen of the United Kingdom of Great Britain and Ireland, His Majesty the Emperor of Austria, His Majesty the Emperor of the French, His Majesty the King of Prussia, His Majesty the Emperor of all the Russias, and His Majesty the King of Sardinia, declare the Sublime Porte admitted to participate in the advantages of the public law and system (concert) of Europe. Their Majesties engage, each on his part, to respect the independence and the territorial integrity of the Ottoman Empire; guaranteeing in common the strict observance of that engagement; and will, in consequence, consider any act tending to its violation as a question of general interest.

Article IX His Imperial Majesty the Sultan, having . . . issued a firman which . . . records his generous intentions towards the Christian population of his Empire . . . has resolved to communicate to the Contracting Parties the said firman, emanating spontaneously from his sovereign will. . . . It is clearly understood that it cannot, in any case, give to the said Powers the right to interfere, either collectively or separately, in the relations of His Majesty the Sultan with his subjects, nor in the internal administration of his Empire.

Article XI The Black Sea is neutralized: its water and its ports, thrown open to the mercantile marine of every nation, are formally and in perpetuity interdicted to the flag of war, either of the Powers possessing its coasts, or of any other Power . . .

Article XIII The Black Sea being neutralized according to the terms of Article XI the maintenance or establishment upon its coasts of military-maritime arsenals become alike unnecessary and purposeless, in consequence, His Majesty the Emperor of all the Russias, and His Imperial Majesty the Sultan engage not to establish or to maintain upon that coast any military-maritime arsenal. . .

Parliamentary Papers lxi (1856) 21–7.

document 53

The War with China

(a) Cobden proposes a vote of censure

... Disavow the acts of your representatives in this miserable affair of the *Arrow* ... you will be disappointed if you think that you will be repaid by increased commerce for the employment of violence ... are these people so barbarous that we should attempt to coerce them by force into granting what we wish? Here is an empire in which is the only relic of the oldest civilization of the world – one which 2,700 years ago ... had a system of primary education – which had its system of logic before the time of Aristotle and its code of morals before that of Socrates.... You find them carrying on their industry in foreign countries with that assiduity and labouriousness which characterize the Scotch and the Swiss ... If in speaking of them we stigmatize them as barbarians, and threaten them with force because we say they are in-accessible to reason, it must be because we do not understand them; because their ways are not our ways, nor our ways theirs.

Hansard, 3rd ser., cxliv, 1419–21 (26 February 1857)

(b) Disraeli challenges Palmerston to hold a general election on the issue

... There is one idea too prevalent with regard to China, – namely, that all England has to do is to act with energy in order to produce the same results as have been achieved in India ... but since the time when our Clives and Hastings founded our Indian Empire the position of affairs in the East has greatly changed. Great Powers have been brought into contact with us in the East. We have the Russian Empire and the American Republic there, and a system of political compromise had developed itself like the balance of power in Europe ... if you have peace with Persia you will probably have succeeded in establishing Russian ascendancy in that country by your violent conduct; while in China, where also you may soon have peace, you will very probably have established the ascendancy of the United States...

Let the noble Lord not only complain to the country, but let him appeal to the country. I hope my constituents will return me again; if they do not, I shall be most happy to meet him on the hustings at Tiverton. I should like to see the programme of the proud leader of the Liberal party – 'No Reform! New Taxes! Canton Blazing! Persia Invaded!' That would be the programme of the statesman who appeals to a great nation as the worthy leader of the cause of progress and civilisation.

Hansard, 3rd ser., cxliv, 1836–7, 1840 (3 March 1857)

document 54

The Italian Question: Palmerston's dilemma

(a) Palmerston to Granville

As for myself, I am very Austrian north of the Alps, but very anti-Austrian south of the Alps. The Austrians have no business in Italy, and they are a public nuisance there. They govern their own provinces ill, and are the props and encouragers of bad government in all the other states of the Peninsula, except in Piedmont, where fortunately they have no influence . . . I should therefore rejoice and feel relieved if Italy up to the Tyrol were freed from Austrian dominion and military occupation. But in politics as in other matters, it is not enough to show a desirable end; one must always be able to point out means of arriving at it, the objectionable nature of which shall not counter-balance the advantage of the result to be accomplished. . .

A war begun to drive the Austrians out of Italy would infallibly succeed in its immediate object, but it might and probably would lead to other consequences much to be deplored. It is greatly for the interests of Europe that Austria should continue to be a great Power in the centre of the Continent; but if she was deeply engaged in a conflict in Italy, the Hungarians would rise, and Russia would threaten on the Galician frontier, and instead of seeing Italy freed, and nothing more, we might find Austria dismembered. But even if this were not to be, the bloodshed and destruction of life and property consequent upon such a war would far more than counter-balance the good that would be accomplished. I hope from what you say that the Emperor Napoleon will be overruled and that peace will be maintained; but if war should unfortunately break out, I am quite sure the only course for England is neutrality. We must stand aloof. Public opinion would not allow the Government to declare war against France, Sardinia, and Russia, in order to maintain Austria in Italy, and of course it is out of the question that we should take part against Austria.

Palmerston to Lord Granville, 30 January 1859; quoted in E. Fitzmaurice, *Life of the Second Lord Granville*, Longmans, Green, 1905, i, 325–6.

But he spoke more decisively during the election campaign of 1859.

(b) Palmerston to the electors of Tiverton

... We were told yesterday that war had actually begun.... Nobody that I am aware of meant to wrest from Austria the territories in Venice and in Lombardy which she possesses by virtue of the treaties of 1815. Those possessions are hers by right; the judgement of Europe affirms that she is entitled to keep them. I do not say the sympathies of Europe, because unfortunately her system of governing those provinces has been such that no man can deny that the discontent which prevails among the people of those countries is justified by the maladministration of Austria since she has possessed them. (Cheers) ... [*Austria's possession of them*] has been a source of infinite misery to the people of the whole peninsula. For Austria ... exerted influence over ... all the other States of Italy from the Po down to the Mediterranean by which in all those countries from that time to this the most abominable system of misgovernment has been supported by the confidence which their Governments felt that, if the just discontent of their subjects should at any period break out into open resistance, Austria was there by overwhelming military force to compel obedience (Cheers). ... If she has invaded Sardinia, she has broken the treaties on which she rests as the security for her own possessions ... if the consequence of Austria's aggression should be that she should be compelled to withdraw north of the Alps and leave Italy free to the Italians, why, however much one may deplore the disastrous calamities by which that result may be obtained, still every generous mind will feel that sometimes out of evil good may flow ...

The Times, 30 April 1859

THE AMERICAN CIVIL WAR

document 55

Cobden on why British opinion was confused

... The English people have no sympathy with you on either side. You know how ignorant we are on the details of your history, geography, constitution, etc. There are two subjects on which we are unanimous and fanatical —personal freedom and Free Trade. These convictions are the result of fifty years of agitation and discussion. In your case we observe a mighty quarrel: on the one side protectionists, on the other slave-owners. The protectionists say they do not seek to put down slavery. The slave-owners say they want Free Trade. Need you wonder at the confusion in John Bull's poor head? He gives it up!

Cobden to Charles Sumner (the Chairman of the U.S. Senate's Foreign Relations Committee), 3 December 1861; quoted in (46) p. 350.

document 56

Gladstone on the strength of the South

Gladstone in common with many other men was convinced that the South would make good its secession.

. . . We known quite well that the people of the Northern states have not yet drunk the cup – they are still trying to hold it far from their lips – which all the rest of the world see they nevertheless must drink of. We may have our own opinions about slavery; we may be for or against the South; but there is no doubt that Jefferson Davis and other leaders of the South have made an army; they are making, it appears, a navy; and they have made what is more than either, they have made a nation.

Gladstone's speech at Newcastle-upon-Tyne, 7 October 1862; quoted in (65), iii, 79.

document 57

The Trent Case

The Prince Consort persuaded the British government to tone down their despatch complaining of the Americans' conduct in removing Mason and Slidell from the Trent.

The Queen returns these important drafts, which upon the whole she approves, but she cannot help feeling that the main draft, that for communication to the American Government, is somewhat meagre. She would have liked to have seen the expression of a hope that the American captain did not act under instructions, or, if he did, that he misapprehended them – that the United States Government must be fully aware that the British Government could not allow its flag to be insulted, and the security of her mail communications to be placed to jeopardy, and Her Majesty's Government are unwilling to believe that the United States Government intended wantonly to put an insult upon this country, and to add to their many distressing complications by forcing a question of dispute upon us, and we are therefore glad to believe that upon a full consideration of the circumstances, and of the undoubted breach of international law committed, they would spontaneously offer such redress as alone could satisfy this country, viz. the restoration of the unfortunate passengers and a suitable apology.

[*Note in the Queen's handwriting*] This draft was the last the beloved Prince ever wrote . . .

Queen Victoria to Earl Russell, 1 December 1861; *Letters of Queen Victoria, 1837–1861*, Murray, 1908, iii, 469–70.

Poland

document 58

Palmerston on the dangers of a Congress

Palmerston refused Napoleon III's suggestion of a Congress on Poland because he feared it might lead to a general revision of the Treaty of Vienna.

Our answer to the Emperor's proposal has been, in substance, that we do not admit that the Treaties of Vienna have ceased to be in force, inasmuch as, on the contrary, they are still the basis of the existing arrangements of Europe; that, with regard to the proposed Congress, before we can come to any decision about it, we should like to know what subjects it is to discuss, and what power it is to possess to give effect to its decisions. . .

My own impression is that the Congress will never meet, and that the Emperor has no expectations that it should meet. The truth is that the assembling of a Congress is not a measure applicable to the present state of Europe. In 1815 a Congress was a necessity. France had overrun all Europe, had overthrown almost all the former territorial arrangements, and had established a new order of things. . . . Nothing of the kind exists in the present state of Europe. There are no doubts as to who is the owner of any piece of territory, and there are not even any boundary questions in dispute . . .

But if the Congress were to enter upon the wide field of proposed and possible changes of territory, what squabbles and animosities would ensue! Russia would ask to get back all she lost by the Treaty of Paris: Italy would ask for Venetia and Rome; France would plead geography for the frontier of the Rhine; Austria would show how advantageous it would be to Turkey to transfer to Austria Bosnia or Moldo-Wallachia; Greece would have a word to say about Thessaly and Epirus; Spain would wonder how England could think of retaining Gibraltar; Denmark would say that Sleswig is geographically part of Jutland, and that, as Jutland is an integral part of Denmark, so ought Sleswig to be so too; Sweden would claim Finland; and some of the greater German states would strongly urge the expediency of mediatizing a score of the smaller Princes. . .

Palmerston to King Leopold of the Belgians, 15 November 1863; quoted in (7), ii, 236—42.

document 59

The Schleswig-Holstein question: Palmerston's 'not England alone' speech

. . . There is no use disguising the fact that what is at the bottom of the German design, and the desire of connecting Schleswig with Holstein, is the dream of a German fleet, and the wish to get Kiel as a German seaport. There may be a good reason why they should wish it, but it is no reason why they should violate the rights and independence of Denmark. . . The hon. Gentleman asks what is the policy and course of Her Majesty's Government with regard to that dispute. As I have already said, we concur entirely with him, and I am satisfied with all reasonable men in Europe, including those in France and Russia, in desiring that the independence, the integrity and the rights of Denmark may be maintained. We are convinced — I am convinced at least — that if any violent attempt were made to overthrow those rights and interfere with that independence, those who made the attempt would find in the result, that it would not be Denmark alone with which they would have to contend. I trust, however, that these transactions will continue to be, as they have been, matters for negotiation, and not for an appeal to arms.

Hansard, 3rd ser., clxxii, 1252 (23 July 1863).

document 60

Palmerston's view on Germany's future

Palmerston always showed less sympathy for German than for Italian nationalism but he did not underestimate the importance of Prussia in the European balance. In 1865 he feared the aggressive tendencies of France and Russia, not of Germany.

It was dishonest and unjust to deprive Denmark of Sleswig and Holstein. It is another question how those two Duchies, when separated from Denmark, can be disposed of best for the interest of Europe. I should say that, with that view, it is better that they should go to increase the power of Prussia than that they should form another little state to be added to the cluster of small bodies politic which encumber Germany, and render it of less force than it ought to be in the general balance of power in the world. Prussia is too weak as she now is ever to be honest or independent in her action; and, with a view to the future, it is desirable that Germany, in the aggregate, should be strong, in order to control those two ambitious and aggressive powers, France and Russia, that press upon her west and east. As to France, we know how restless and aggressive she is, and how ready to break loose for Belgium, for the Rhine, for anything she would be likely to get without too much exertion. As to Russia, she will, in due time, become a power almost as great as the old Roman Empire. She can become mistress of all Asia, except British India, whenever she chooses to take it; and when enlightened arrangements shall have made her revenue proportioned to her territory, and railways shall have abridged distances, her command of men will become enormous, her pecuniary means gigantic, and her power of transporting armies over great distances most formidable. Germany ought to be strong in order to resist Russian aggression, and a strong Prussia is essential to German strength. Therefore, though I heartily condemn the whole of the proceedings of Austria and Prussia about the Duchies, I own that I should rather see them incorporated with Prussia than converted into an additional asteroid in the system of Europe.

Palmerston to Russell, 13 September 1865; quoted in (7), ii, 270–1.

Bibliography

(The place of publication is London unless otherwise stated.)

1 Aberdeen, Earl of, ed. E. Jones Parry. *The Correspondence of Lord Aberdeen and Princess Lieven*, Camden Society, 3rd ser., Nos 60, 62, Royal Historical Society, 1938–9.

2 Adams, E.D. *Great Britain and the American Civil War*, 2 vols, Russell & Russell, New York, 1925.

3 Albrecht-Carrié, R. 'The Concert of Europe' (in *Documentary History of Western Civilisation*, eds. E.C. Black and L.W. Levy), Macmillan, 1968.

4 Allen, H.C. *Great Britain and the United States: a history of Anglo-American relations, 1883–1952*, Odhams Press, 1954.

5 Anderson, M.S. *The Eastern Question, 1774–1923*, Macmillan, 1966: the only modern comprehensive study of this question.

6 Anderson, M.S. *The Great Powers and the Near East, 1774–1923* (documents), Edward Arnold, 1970.

7 Ashley, Evelyn. *The Life of Henry John Temple, Viscount Palmerston, 1846–1865*, 2 vols, Bentley & Son, 1876: the continuation of **(21)**.

8 Bartlett, C.J. *Great Britain and Sea Power, 1815–1853*, Oxford University Press, 1963.

9 Bartlett, C.J. *Castlereagh*, Macmillan, 1966.

10 Bartlett, C.J., ed. *Britain Pre-Eminent*, Macmillan, 1969.

11 Beales, Derek, *England and Italy, 1859–1860*, Nelson, 1961.

12 Beasley, W.G. *Great Britain and the opening of Japan, 1834–1858*, Luzac, 1951.

13 Bell, H.C.F. *Lord Palmerston*, 2 vols, Longmans, Green, 1936.

14 Bernard, Mountague. *A historical account of the neutrality of Great Britain during the American Civil War* (1870), reprinted Burt Franklin, New York, 1971.

15 Bindoff, S.T. 'The unreformed Diplomatic Service, 1812–1860', *Transactions of the Royal Historical Society*, 4th ser., xviii (1935), 143–72.

16 Bourne, K. *Britain and the Balance of Power in North America, 1815–1908*, Longmans, 1967.

17 Bourne, K. and Watt, D.C. *Studies in International History*, Longmans, 1967.

18 Bourne, K. *The Foreign Policy of Victorian England, 1830–1902* (documents), Clarendon Press, Oxford, 1970.

19 Brebner, J.B. *The Atlantic Triangle: the interplay of Canada, the United States and Great Britain*, Carnegie, New Haven, 1947.

20 Bullen, R. *Palmerston, Guizot and the Collapse of the Entente Cordiale*, Athlone Press, 1974.

21 Bulwer, H.L. (Baron Dalling). *The Life of Henry John Temple, Viscount Palmerston* (to 1846), 3 vols, Bentley & Son, 1871–74.

22 *Cambridge History of British Foreign Policy, 1783–1919*, eds. Sir A. Ward and G.P. Gooch, 3 vols, Cambridge University Press, 1922–3.

23 Carr, W. *Schleswig-Holstein, 1815–1848*, Manchester University Press, 1963.

24 Conacher, J.B. *The Aberdeen Coalition, 1852–1855*, Cambridge University Press, 1968.

25 Connell, B. *Regina v. Palmerston: the correspondence between Queen Victoria and her Foreign and Prime Minister, 1837–1865*, Evans Bros, 1962.

26 Costin, W. *Great Britain and China, 1833–1860* (1937), reprinted Clarendon Press, Oxford, 1968.

27 Crawley, C.W. *The Question of Greek Independence: a study of British Foreign Policy, 1821–1833*, Cambridge University Press, 1930.

28 Derry, J.W. *Castlereagh*, Allen Lane, 1976.

29 Duhamel, J. *Louis-Philippe et la première entente cordiale*, Pierre Horay, Paris, 1951.

30 Edwardes, Michael, *Playing the Great Game: a Victorian Cold War*, Hamish Hamilton, 1975.

31 Ehrman, John, *The Younger Pitt: the years of acclaim*, Constable 1969.

32 Eyck, Erich (trans. E. Northcott). *Pitt versus Fox: father and son, 1735–1806*, G. Bell and Sons, 1950.

33 Fitzmaurice, E. *The Life of Granville George Leveson Gower, Second Earl Granville*, 2 vols, Longmans, 1905.

34 Flournoy, F.R. *British Policy towards Morocco in the Age of Palmerston, 1830–1865*, P.S. King, 1935.

35 Gillard, David. *The Struggle for Asia, 1828–1914: a study in British and Russian imperialism*, Methuen, 1977.

36 Gordon, Sir Arthur (Lord Stanmore), *The Earl of Aberdeen*, Sampson Low, 1893.

37 Graubaud, S.R. 'Castlereagh and the Peace of Europe', *Journal of British Studies*, iii (1963), pp. 79–87.

38 Gregory, J. S. *Great Britain and the Taipings*, Routledge & Kegan Paul, 1969.

39 Guedella, P. *Palmerston*, Benn, 1926.

40 Gulick, E.V. *Europe's Classical Balance of Power*, Cornell University Press, New York, 1955.

41 Guyot, R. *La Première entente cordiale*, Paris, 1926.

42 Hall, John. *England and the Orleans Monarchy*, Smith Elder, 1912.

43 Helleiner, Karl F. *The Imperial Loans: a study in financial and diplomatic history*, Clarendon Press, Oxford, 1965.

44 Henderson, G.B. *Crimean War Diplomacy and other essays*, Jackson, Glasgow, 1947.

45 Hinde, Wendy, *George Canning*, Collins, 1973.

46 Hobson, J.A. *Richard Cobden: the international man* (1919), new edition (introduction by N. Masterman), Benn, 1968.

47 Hodder, Edwin, *Life and Work of the Seventh Earl of Shaftesbury K.G.*, 3 vols, Cassell, 1887.

48 Holbraad, C. *The Concert of Europe: a study in German and British international theory, 1815–1914*, Longman, 1970.

49 Hoskins, H.L. *British Routes to India* (1928), reprinted Cass, 1968.

50 Howard, C. *Splendid Isolation*, Macmillan, 1967.

51 Howard, C. *Britain and the Casus Belli*, Athlone Press, 1974.

52 Imlah, A.G. *Britain and Switzerland, 1845–1860*, Longmans, 1966.

53 Ingle, H.H. *Nesselrode and the Russian rapprochement with Britain, 1836–1844*, University of California Press, Berkeley, 1976.

54 Jarrett, Derek, *Pitt the Younger* (introduction by A.J.P. Taylor), Weidenfeld & Nicolson, 1974.

55 Jones, Ray, *The Nineteenth Century Foreign Office: an administrative history*, Weidenfeld & Nicolson, 1971.

56 Kelly, John B. *Britain and the Persian Gulf, 1795–1880*, Clarendon Press, Oxford, 1968.

57 Kissinger, H. *A World Restored, 1812–1822*, Grosset & Dunlap, New York, 1957.

58 Lambert, S. Review article of the reissue of *A Century of Diplomatic Blue Books, Historical Journal* x (1967), 125–31: an up-to-date criticism of this important tool of diplomatic history.

59 Lane-Poole, Stanley, *Life of Stratford Canning*, 2 vols, Longmans, 1888.

60 Longford, Lady, *Wellington: the years of the sword* and *Wellington: pillar of state*, Weidenfeld & Nicolson, 1969, 1972.

61 Marlowe, J. *Perfidious Albion: the origins of Anglo-French rivalry in the Levant*, Elek, 1971.

62 Martin, B. Kingsley, *The Triumph of Lord Palmerston*, Allen & Unwin, 1924.

139

63 Maxwell, Sir Herbert, *The Life and Letters of George William Frederick, Fourth Earl of Clarendon*, 2 vols, Edward Arnold, 1913.

64 Morley, John, *Life of Richard Cobden*, Chapman & Hall, 1881.

65 Morley, John, *Life of Gladstone*, 3 vols, Macmillan, 1903.

66 Mosse, W.E. *The European Powers and the German Question, 1848–1871*, Cambridge University Press, 1958.

67 Mosse, W.E. *The Rise and Fall of the Crimean System, 1855–1871*, Macmillan, 1963.

68 Nicolson, H. *The Congress of Vienna: a study in allied unity, 1812–1822* (1946), reprinted Methuen, 1961.

69 Nicolson, H. *Diplomacy*, 3rd edn, Oxford University Press, 1965.

70 Parry, E. Jones-. *The Spanish Marriages, 1841–1846*, Macmillan, 1936.

71 Perkins, Bradford. *Castlereagh and Adams: England and the United States, 1812–1823*, University of California Press, Berkeley, 1964.

72 Platt, D.C.M. *Finance, Trade and Politics in British Foreign Policy, 1815–1914*, Oxford University Press, 1968.

73 Porter, B. *The Lion's Share: a short history of British imperialism, 1850–1970*, Longman, 1975.

74 Prest, J. *Lord John Russell*, Macmillan, 1972.

75 Puryear, V.J. *England, Russia and the Straits Question, 1844–1856*, University of California, Berkeley, 1931.

76 Puryear, V.J. *International Economics and Diplomacy in the Near East, 1834–1853*, Stanford University Press, 1935.

77 Renier, G.J. *Great Britain and the Establishment of the kingdom of the Netherlands 1813–1815: a study in British foreign policy*, Martinus Nijhoff, The Hague, 1930.

78 Ridley, Jasper, *Lord Palmerston*, Constable, 1970.

79 Rolo, P.J.V. *George Canning: three biographical studies*, Macmillan, 1965.

80 Rose, J. Holland. *Napoleonic Studies*, George Bell & Sons, 1904.

81 Russell, Lord John. *Selections from the Speeches of Earl Russell 1817 to 1841 and from Despatches 1859 to 1865 . . .*, 2 vols, Longmans, 1870.

82 Russell, Lord John (ed. G.P. Gooch). *The Later Correspondence of Lord John Russell, 1840–1878*, Longmans, 1925.

83 Seton-Watson, R.W. *Britain in Europe, 1789–1914*, Cambridge University Press, 1945.

84 Sproxton, C. *Palmerston and the Hungarian Revolution*, Cambridge University Press, 1919.

85 Steefel, L. *The Schleswig-Holstein Question*, Harvard Historical Series, Cambridge, Mass., 1932.

86 Sudley, Lord (trans. and ed.). *The Lieven-Palmerston Correspondence. 1828–1856*, John Murray, 1943.

87 Taylor, A.J.P. *The Italian Problem in European Diplomacy, 1847–1849*, Manchester University Press, 1934.

88 Taylor, A.J.P. *The Struggle for the Mastery in Europe, 1848–1918*, Clarendon Press Oxford, 1954.

89 Taylor, A.J.P. *The Trouble Makers: dissent over foreign policy, 1792–1939*, Hamish Hamilton, 1957.

90 Temperley, H.W.V. *Life of Canning*, James Finch, 1905.

91 Temperley, H.W.V. *The Foreign Policy of Canning, 1822–1827: England, the neo-Holy Alliance and the New World* (1925), reprinted (new introduction by H. Butterfield) Cass, 1966.

92 Temperley, H.W.V. *England and the Near East: the Crimea* (1936), reprinted Cass, 1964.

93 Temperley, H. and Penson, L.M. *The Foundations of British Foreign Policy from Pitt (1792) to Salisbury (1902)*, Cambridge University Press, 1938.

94 Temperley, H.W.V. and Penson, L.M. *A Century of Diplomatic Blue Books 1814–1914* (1938), new edition Cass, 1966.

95 Watson, J. Steven, *The Reign of George III, 1760–1815* (Oxford History of England), Clarendon Press, Oxford, 1960.

96 Webster, C.K. *The Congress of Vienna, 1814–1815;* reprinted Thames & Hudson, 1963.

97 Webster, C.K. *British Diplomacy, 1813–1815* (documents), G. Bell & Sons, 1921.

98 Webster, C.K. *The Foreign Policy of Castlereagh, 1815–1822: Britain and the European Alliance*, G. Bell & Sons, 1925.

99 Webster, C.K. *The Foreign Policy of Castlereagh, 1812–1815: Britain and the reconstruction of Europe*, G. Bell & Sons, 1931.

100 Webster, C.K. *Britain and the Independence of Latin America, 1812–1830*, Oxford University Press, 1944.

101 Webster, C.K. *The Foreign Policy of Palmerston, 1830–1841*, 2 vols, G. Bell & Sons, 1951.

102 Webster, C.K. *The Art and Practice of Diplomacy*, Chatto and Windus, 1961.

103 Woodward, E.L. *The Age of Reform, 1815–1870* (Oxford History of England), Clarendon Press, Oxford, 1938.

Index